THE TENT OF MEETING

TEXTS

Published by THE TENT OF MEETING, P.O. Box 8518, Santa Fe, NM 87504
Printed in the United States of America
ISBN 0-9615531-0-3

With thanks to Marina Warner © for permission to publish *Lady Wisdom,* from her new book,
The Eyes of Tieresias.

Thanks to Dr. Vera John Steiner and Prof. Mark Rutledge, Director of Campus Ministries of the
University of New Mexico for making Dr. Steiner's article available to us for this volume.

Thanks to Steven Lowe of *Casa Sin Nombre* for the typesetting.

Cover Art by Charles Ramsburg.

THANKS

My first acknowledgement must be to Michele Zackheim whose idea for *The Tent of Meeting* included a book and who thoughtfully invited me to undertake this aspect of the project.

To Anna Walton for editorial assistance and to Sarah Stanley and Suzanne Vilmain for talented work on production, much appreciation is due.

And special thanks are owed and cheerfully given to Mr. and Mrs. Charles Ramsburg, Jr. of Sewickley, PA . . .whose generous grant made this publication possible.

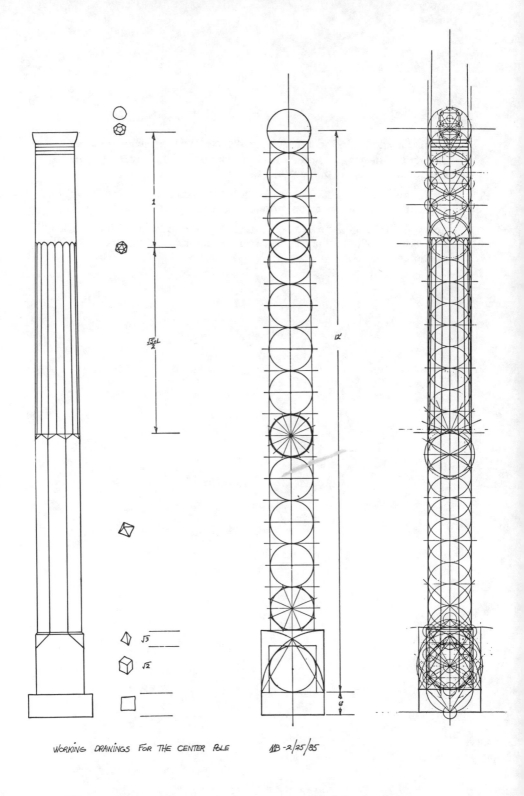

WORKING DRAWINGS FOR THE CENTER POLE   MB - 2/25/85

CENTER POLE

The center pole shown on the facing page in a drawing actually functions both as a pole for supporting the "Tent" canopy and as a mast by which this canopy is raised to position. It was designed and constructed in collaboration with Keith Critchlow, by the Lindisfarne Artisans Guild.

Standing and acting as it does, symbolically with "feet on earth and head in heaven," it expresses much of the idea of humanity as embodied in the three Abrahamic traditions.

The pole itself rests on a square plinth. Classically, the square represented the basis, context and domain of fundamental activity. The four qualities of matter (fire, air, water, earth), the four directions, the four seasons, etc., are examples of this idea.

On top of the plinth rests a cube which signifies the "earth" of being human. As a solid with six planes, it has long been employed as symbol of the six dimensions (three of time and three of space) and the six days of creation. The cube also is the expression of its implicit interior center point reflecting the seventh day, the mysteriousness of the day of rest and completion.

The four planes of the cube extend upward, pair off, and begin setting out in three-dimensional language the poetry of the laws of generation. Please refer to the drawing while reading what follows.

The first generation reveals four equilateral triangles which then form an octagonal base. The base modulates to an eight-sided column which then extends up by nine intervals to the next transition; an octave from eight to sixteen.

At this level the pole begins a subtle taper of one degree ($\frac{1}{360}$th of a circle), and rises to the next level of transition where arcs, petals, or feathers (choose your preferred metaphor) change the sixteen-sided column into a circular drum.

The drum rises four intervals, finally to articulate three bands, or rings, which then form a fourth and chalice.

Here we move from the seen to the unseen, from the explicit to the implicit. The dimensions of the cup at the top of the pole (shown in drawing) and its deliberate "vessel-ness," i.e., a calling to be filled to fully be itself, suggest to a careful study the presence of a sphere.

Michael Baron

To L.R.

EDITOR'S PREFACE

This book is made of varied pieces of writing by a group of people in sympathy with the undertaking implicit in THE TENT OF MEETING project.

Like most of us they have grown up in cultures seeded, matriced and generated by at least one of the three major monotheistic religions. Territory common to us is belief in one God. Our feet reach common ground also in the view that human nature is radically authentic in its being and gifted with the potential to act from a free will. Then too, we put a high value on speech as an act of freedom.

Because of the limited number of months available for preparation, I as editor, gave "time and chance" a prime place in the method of soliciting text for the book. What we have here figuratively speaking, are voices of people who have walked into a tent at a particular time and were invited to say something. But since each contributor speaks as a free subject, that time is neither everybody's nor an abstraction. It is his or her time; his or her place.

I call attention to time and place so emphatically because a fresh and open approach to these conceptions is helpful toward appreciating this somewhat idiosyncratic volume. The notion of a tent in these days usually calls to mind a temporary dwelling in a location a bit off the beaten track.

In a sense the text of this book is an invitation to step outside our customary brackets and to remember what our world of technical and mental artifacts presses us to forget. The time we usually run by is "of the clock," not the "time" of the world that is the dwelling of these three great traditions. We may recall that Abraham stepped away from the visionary and technical systems current in Ur of the Chaldees to seek and find God.

Some articles are long, some short. Some contributors are speaking from within a highly traditional context while others are not. Also, as I have said there is no obvious or explicit theme. One may emerge for the reader; but to have imposed one on the contributors would have re-bracketted them, and would have been opposed to the spirit of the undertaking.

Being human offers the chance to bear witness to the worth of the place where one stands. Whether it is called Mikdash, Kaaba, Cross, or world, the "place" is implicitly infinite.

You, as reader, will find diverse content, shape and size among the articles; but each will reward a careful reading.

I hope this small book is like a "tent flap," the "wings of a tent," a Ruba'iyat, through which many of us can enter into a dialogue brimming with listening and silence and speech.

John Menken

TABLE OF CONTENTS

THE TENT OF MEETING WITHIN
Paul Mendes-Flohr 11

TIME AND PRAYER
Father Hilary Thimmesh 15

A LIFE
Sahag Kalaydjian 20

BEYOND ABSOLUTIST IDEOLOGIES
Colin Williams 23

DESERT MONKS—EUROPEAN BEDOUIN
Dan Rabinowitz 30

THE CARMELITE STORY
Mother Tessa Bielecki and Father William McNamara, O.C.D. . . 41

THE SHIP OF SAFETY
Sheikh Mohammed Sayad Al Jemal Al Rifai Ash-Shadhulli 51

NECESSARY QUESTIONS
John Menken 62

IS OUR NEIGHBOR VISIBLE?
Dr. Vera John-Steiner 66

LADY WISDOM
Marina Warner 71

PRINCIPALITIES AND POWER
Lynne Bundesen 105

VIENNESE COYOTE
Richard Erdoes 109

HOW SHALL I WRITE?
A Bedouin 120

I AM A STRANGER IN THE LAND
Rabbi Michael Goldberg 125

THE SAME MESSAGE REPEATED
Mohammed H. El-Zayyat 129

LISTEN ISRAEL
Andre Chouraque 133

BIOGRAPHIES 136

THE TENT OF MEETING WITHIN

Paul Mendes-Flohr

Several years ago I had the occasion to accompany a Bedouin friend on a visit to his relatives in the Negev Desert of Israel. Upon our arrival at the encampment we were cordially ushered into the main tent where we were joined by Mohammed's male relatives whom my friend had not seen since he was a child. (The women entertained Mohammed's wife, Jamillah, in a separate tent.) After a ceremonious exchange of salutations, we were seated on a lavish carpet, served fragrant tea, and then pungent coffee. No one spoke. As the seemingly endless silence continued, I became nervous and self-conscious. I thought that perhaps I should be the gallant one to "break the ice," and mumbled some harmless inanity about the weather and the goats peering inquisitively into the tent. Someone politely nodded, but I failed to provoke conversation. The silence persisted. After about an hour, Mohammed and his relatives suddenly arose and graciously bade each other farewell.

Only in retrospect, when invited by the editor of this volume to share my reflections on the Tent of Meeting as a symbol of ecumenical dialogue, did I begin to understand what occurred in the reticent reunion of Mohammed's family. It was a "tent of meeting." Like the biblical Tent of Meeting which was established to allow Moses to encounter God—"the Tent of Meeting where I will meet with you" (Exodus 30:36)—the canopy of silence erected by Muhammed and his desert hosts was designed to facilitate their mutual meeting. It was a meeting uncluttered by speech, undisturbed by words that deflect genuine attention to each other. This silence, as the people of the desert in their ancient wisdom ap-

11

parently understand it, is meant to encourage us to be comfortable with each other's presence—not just the abstract idea or image of each other, but the concrete, abiding reality of each other. In the Canopy of Silence we behold in meditative respect the concrete presence of each other, the distinctive lines experience has etched on our faces, the individual shape of our hands, the rhythm of our breathing . . .

Echoing the stillness of the desert, silence is the language of hospitality —or as the biblical Hebrew of the nomadic Israelites expresses the act of greeting in one's home a guest or stranger, *hakhnasat orhim*, "bringing the guest into one's home," or personal space. In silence, the bedouin meets the stranger-become-guest, suspending not only speech but judgment and perhaps prejudice as well, and learns to accept the presence and details that define the other.

The philosopher Martin Buber avers that "all real living is meeting," a learning to meet each other not as an object of thought or instrumental aim, but as a unique, intrinsically dignified presence. Buber suggests that when we learn to meet the presence, "the Thou," of each other we also meet the presence of God, "the Eternal Thou." As the biblical Tent of Meeting provided a "sanctuary" (in Hebrew, *mishkan,* literally, a dwelling) for God, so the Divine Presence dwells in the tent of meeting in which we humans are to meet each other.

Perhaps it is not sheer coincidence that I have chosen to write this essay on the morrow of the Sabbath during which Jews read in the synagogue the Torah portion dealing with the Tent of Meeting and its construction (Exodus 25:1-27:19). In their commentary on this Sabbath reading, the rabbinic sages throughout the generations have emphasized God's instructions to Moses to solicit from the children of Israel gifts for the building of the sanctuary :

The Lord spoke to Moses, saying "Tell the Israelite people to bring Me gifts; you shall accept gifts for Me from every person whose heart so moves him."

Exodus 25:1-2
(New Jewish Publication Society translation)

As the rabbis comment, God, of course, did not need the gifts of "gold, silver and copper" from the people whom He had only just redeemed from Egyptian bondage and to whom He gave the Torah. Then why did He command Moses to collect these gifts? The rabbis point out that the key passage in which God called for gifts " from every person whose heart so moves him" *(yedivenu libo)* is derived from the Hebrew reflexive verb *(hitnadev)*, often used in the Bible to designate "a giving of oneself" (See Judges 5:9; Ezra 3:5 and 1 Chronicles 29:5). God wants more than generosity or philanthropy; He demands involvement and commitment. Hence, by beseeching the people of Israel to contribute "from their hearts" to construction of the Tent of Meeting, He sought to convert them from *passive recipients* of His gracious gifts into *active partners* in the task of bringing holiness into the world. For the rabbis the Tent of Meeting symbolizes this partnership:

> And let them make me a Sanctuary
> that I may dwell among them.
>
> Exodus 25:8

The Israelites *made* the Sanctuary in which God met them. The Tent of Meeting is thus the message of divine love, and a promise of intimate partnership with him.

In the "tent of meeting" between peoples each of us is a partner in its ultimate construction; we are implored by the biblical origins of the symbol not to suffice with a passive, aesthetic appreciation of the idea of meeting. We are beckoned to be active partners in its genuine, not just symbolic, construction. Here the task is immeasurably more difficult than its artistic construction, notwithstanding the magnificence of this achievement. For as the rabbis also remind us, the Tent of Meeting was built not only so that God will dwell within it, but among us:

> And let them make me a sanctuary
> that I may dwell among them.
>
> Exodus 25:8

Reflecting on this verse, a sixteenth century rabbi of Gorizia, Italy, commented:

> . . .the text does not say 'that I may dwell in its midst' (*be-tokho)*, but 'among them' (*be-tokham)*, to teach you that the Divine Presence does not rest upon the sanctuary by virtue of the sanctuary itself but by virtue of Israel, 'for *they* are the temple of the Lord.'

In his commentary on this very same passage, the nineteenth century Russian rabbi, Malbim, further observed:

> God commanded that each individual should build Him a sanctuary in the recesses of his heart, that he should prepare himself to be a dwelling place for the Lord and a stronghold for the excellency of His Presence, as well as an altar on which to offer up every portion of his soul to the Lord, until he gives himself for his glory at all times.

We are told that the great hasidic master, Rabbi Menahem Mendel of Kotzk (d.1859) once surprised a gathering of learned men by suddenly asking "Where is the dwelling of God?" They dismissed his seemingly naive question with laughter. "What a thing to ask! Is not the whole world full of His glory?" The Rabbi of Kotzk then answered his own question: "God dwells wherever we let Him in."

Similarly, the Tent of Meeting that Michele Zackheim beckons us to enter is not confined to this exhibit and the occasion of our visit to it. The meeting that occurs in this place—the silent learning to feel comfortable with the presence of other religious traditions than our own—is to help prepare us to create a tent of meeting within and between ourselves, a tent which we are to establish ever anew as we make our passage through life.

Paul Mendes-Flohr
Jerusalem
Adar 5745/February 1985

TIME AND PRAYER
Father Hilary Thimmesh

At Senanque, near Gordes, hidden in the foothills of the Vaucluse, east of Avignon, stands a primitive Cistercian monastery. The traveller first sees it from above, from a mountain road winding down into a narrow valley. The plain geometrical forms of the church and cloister block the valley with an unadorned stolidity that has little in common with the architectural glory of later Cistercian foundations such as Rievaulx in Yorkshire.

At Senanque, the original structures are plain and functional in the twelfth-century way. One can prescind from the latter-day additions, picture the fields where the monks once worked, enter the empty church where the afternoon sun warms the undecorated stone, and from the choir mount stairs directly to the dorter where the monks slept in the cloister adjoining the church.

The dorter is a long stone hall without partitions. From it the monks filed after the eighth hour of the night to their places in choir for the long Night Office of psalms and readings. To it they returned from choir at nightfall, having completed the day as they began it with psalmody together in the presence of God.

The flight of stone stairs from dormitory to choir, from choir to dormitory, tells us something about the place of prayer in their life. In varying architectural form these stairs occurred again and again in medieval monasteries throughout Europe. The monks, of course, needed other rooms besides the oratory and the dormitory, although fewer than we might think: a kitchen, a calefactory where one could warm oneself in winter, a refectory, an infirmary, a wash house, a latrine, and various out-buildings. Great establishments required more structures for guests, for students, for the abbot as he became a feudal lord. The Plan of St. Gall shows how complex such a monastery could become.

But I turn back to the model of primitive monasticism at Senanque. An early product of the Cistercian reform, it reflects a determination to return to essentials, to a pattern of life centered in the rhythm of prayer, work, and sleep. The stairs from dorter to choir, choir to dorter, tell the story. Time counted in the Roman fashion, twelve hours of darkness, twelve hours of daylight, and buildings so planned as to make the fullest use of each hour.

The Rule of Benedict, which the Cistercians aimed to follow in its full rigor, sets the monastic schedule from summer to winter, winter to summer, so that dawn finds the monks at prayer and dusk closes on the blessing for sleep. The arrangement of hours between dawn and dusk changes with the coming of the winter, the season of Lent, the longer days of summer; but the balance of time allowed for prayer in choir, prayerful reading, and work holds steady from year-end to year- end. Besides the extended Night Office and the morning prayer of Lauds, short offices of choral prayer punctuated the day at roughly three-hour intervals. The schedule was not inflexible. Work might be extended to as much as six consecutive hours during the growing season. Exceptions to the horarium might be allowed in various cases. But in addition to the times of choral prayer, three or four hours a day were set aside for what we would call private reading, although privacy as we think of it—a room or place apart from others—was alien to conventual life and to medieval life generally. Private reading, nonetheless, is distinct from readings and prayer in common at table and in choir.

It must be understood that this reading was holy reading, *lectio divina*; not a leisurely pastime or an academic pursuit. To call it prayerful reading describes its purpose. It was reading dedicated to pondering and absorbing the Scriptures and the writings of the ancient monks and the Church Fathers. This reading provided the mental sustenance of prayer and was itself prayer according to the words of the psalmist:

> The revelation of your words sheds light, giving
> understanding to the simple (Ps. 119:130).

Ignatius Brianchaniov, reflecting the Russian tradition, tells us that a certain holy monk devoted twenty years to the writings of the Fathers before he considered himself ready to practice the prayer of silence, for, as he observes, to make a thorough study of the Scriptures considerable time is necessary (*On the Prayer of Jesus,* p. 69). From such a study on a given day might come tears, or joy, or the flat truth of self-recognition, or a new awareness of God, or perhaps no discernable gain at all.

All of this may sound quite edifying in theory, but in fact we have a hard time imagining people giving over so much time to prayer. On a rough calculation, something near eight hours out of every twenty-four must have been allotted to the common prayer in choir and to individual prayerful reading. One should not assume that extraordinary states of prayer often occurred or were expected. There is little about ecstasy in monastic literature. Nor should we imagine an atmosphere of ascetical passivity where the goal was to become oblivious of time. The very division of the day into hours tells us that these were our kinsmen, people conscious of schedules and work to be done, fields to be harvested, food to be prepared, guests to be served, the elderly and the infirm to be cared for. What puzzles and gives pause is that so much time was measured out and set aside for prayer, which neither feeds the hungry nor clothes the naked nor provides any economic necessity, but only, surely, takes time.

It cannot have been as simple as it sounds. It is one thing to say one's prayers; another, to devote one's life to prayer. A telling injunction in the Rule of Benedict suggests the difficulty:

> One or two seniors must surely be deputed to make the rounds of the monastery while the brothers are reading. Their duty is to see that no brother is so apathetic as to waste time or engage in idle talk to the neglect of his reading, and so not only harm himself but also distract others (48:17-18)

"To see that no brother is so apathetic." The key word in the Latin text is acediosus. The translator might have said "so bored." How could we suppose that such long hours of prayer day after day were devoid of monotony? The novelty of a strict regimen soon wears off. The would-be holy man risks not discovering God in any recognizable manifestation but only time.

He has yet to know that time is a ceaseless river carrying him to God, in whom a thousand years are as one day. In earth's time the tide rises, edging up the beach, trickling among the rocks, refilling the rock pools where the orange algae grow. The tide ebbs and shore birds run in its receding edge, gathering the harvest of the moist strand. The seasons move in greater tides of heat and cold, thawing and freezing, the earth greening and browning beneath the sun. But to enter this rhythm, to sense this great current of life, to yield in peace to its movement is not accomplished by a single intention or by an iron resolution but only by docility, patience, acceptance.

To overcome the monotony of waiting for God is the great hurdle of prayer: to conquer time, which is to say to conquer the fear of futility. For is not time a commodity given us to use, the more precious because limited, because we age, because our years, however many, are few? This great fear haunted the Renaissance as it does us. It is classically expressed in Shakespeare's sonnets:

> And Time that gave doth now his gift confound.
> Time doth transfix the flourish set on youth
> And delves the parallels in beauty's brow,
> Feeds on the rarities of nature's truth,
> And nothing stands but for his scyth to mow (60:8-12).

In a thousand less romantic forms this materialistic, this fatalistic interpretation of time discourages prayer. There is so much to do, so little time to do it, and in prayer nothing may happen that makes much of time. Nothing is made. There is no product, nothing to show, often enough not even any satisfaction beyond the sense of duty done. At best a certain kind of inner form takes shape, sometimes early, sometimes late. The prayer of the mind, the Russian monks say, descends into the heart. But the result may not be evident to anyone, not even—except obscurely—to the one in whom it takes place.

Why then do it? Why give so much time to prayer? Through the barrier of monotony the monks go from their beds to their choir stalls by the most direct route, seeking not to make something but to discover something. From their psalms to their beds they return at the end of each day. Charles Peguy saw night as God's beautiful daughter and sleep as the image of trust and hope. It is not incidental that sleep and prayer and work are prescribed in balanced proportions in the monastic rule. The rhythm of life can continue in holy and hope-filled monotony while the inner form, the heart, grows humble and empty, like a rock pool awaiting the incoming tide of God.

Does nothing happen in prayer that warrants the time given to it? The response to that question is that no gift is too great in exchange for love. Time is the gift one must give for a love whose form is unknown. Time is the gift within our power. The love which is the object of prayer is not within our power except to seek in thought and desire. Prayer often begins with yearning, desire, some attraction to God remotely or piercingly felt for a moment, but it continues only in patience, in repetitive practice that molds the heart to the psalms, that reveals the meaning of the Scriptures. Augustine marvelled at the twofold quality of the Scriptures, at once so open to all and so rich in continued discovery. "So I dwelt upon these things and You were near me, I sighed and You heard me, I was wavering uncertainly and You guided me..."(Confessions ,VI, 5) In time prayer becomes a matter of conviction rather than feeling, intuition rather than reason, gift rather than accomplishment.

It is instructive to note the affinity between this spiritual doctrine and the awareness to which Shakespeare came in his later sonnets and plays that time may be not the foe of love but its ally and guarantor. Where he had earlier lamented the brevity of life and adopted a conventional fatalism, he now discovered a fuller wisdom.

> Those lines that I before have writ do lie,
> Even those that said I could not love you dearer:
> Yet then my judgement knew no reason why
> My most full flame should afterwards burn clearer   115: 1-4)

Time had appeared to be the enemy of love, but now, "reckoning Time" with its "millioned accidents," he knows that love may grow with time. He knows the hazards of time, "the course of altering things," but has come to the assurance that

> Love's not Time's fool, though rosy lips and cheeks
> Within his bending sickle's compass come. (116:9- 10)

Translated into a perennial philosophy, as it is an example, in *The Winter's Tale*, this wisdom accords with the view of time which the monastic theory assumed. The waiting of prayer, the long and seemingly fruitless hours, the outer monotony which cloaks the slow transformation of expectations, is the way to a love that exceeds all definitions. The Expected One is not who we think. What can be conceptualized is not God. And so we must wait—distracted, bored, and empty much of the time, maybe most of the time—while there comes to birth in us the Unknown, the silent Word.

In the end the monks do not trudge up and down their stairs—to say their prayers, to rest in peace on their beds—for the sake of any esthetic experience or any refined sensibility or any psychological sophistication although all of these may be part of their mental and emotional equipment, but to become receptive to the possibilities of a love beyond time through the medium of hours and days and years given to silent, attentive waiting.

Hilary Thimmesh, OSB
St. John's Abbey

A LIFE

Sahag Kalaydjian

Sahag Kalaydjian was born in Bagdad, Iraq, on the first of January, 1924. For his parents, Missag and Markrid Kalaydjian, he was a tenth child. But before his birth, his parents had lost nine of their children from the 1915 genocide of the Armenians or consequent poverty and illness.They were six daughters and three sons. The family originally came from a small town called Zeytoun in the province of Cilicia, Turkey.

Missag and Markrid had heard that in Jerusalem, in the Cathedral of St. James, was the shrine and tomb of St. James the Major, one of the Apostles of Christ. The saint had been decapitated by order of the Roman Governor, Herodius Agrippus, in Jerusalem in the year 44 A.D. According to tradition the body was thrown into the Mediterranean Sea and the waves carried it to Spain where it is now said to rest at Santiago de Campestello. So, when Sahag was born, his parents made a vow to God to dedicate him to the patron saint of the Armenians, the above mentioned St.James, brother of John the Evangelist.

In Bagdad they baptized him as Isaac, mindful of the sacrifice that Abraham wanted to make to God. At that time, a custom existed (to today) among Armenians, to let sons have long hair like a girl. That is the way Sahag came to Jerusalem, when three months old, with long hair and dedicated to the patron Saint of the Armenians. They were given shelter in the Armenian Convent, Old City, Jerusalem. From the time Sahag was a year old Missag and Markrid took him to Church where his ears were filled with all the songs, chants and melodies of the church. Though he had a keen desire to study music, his parents could not afford it at the time, and he could not. In a special ceremony at the shrine of St. James, his long hair was cut when he was seven years old. This was fulfilling his parents wish that Sahag should be seven years old before his hair was cut.

At St. Tarkmantchatz (Holy Translators) Armenian School he received his elementary education. High school study continued at College des Freres (Brother's College) in Jerusalem. Sahag sat for the Palestine Matriculation Examination, passing all seven subjects and earning distinction in English Language, Armenian, and Mathematics. While at College des Freres, he also received certificates for typing and accountancy.

In 1939 Sahag loses his father. In 1942 he loses his mother.

After receiving his diploma in 1942, he began work at the British Paymasters' Office in Jerusalem and stayed there until October 1947. Then, until May 15, 1948, he worked in Barclays Bank.

Sahag was married in 1951, and the couple have lived in the Armenian Convent until now.

Beginning in 1949, he has been the choir-director of the Armenian Church in Jerusalem, and also since 1951, he is the Secretary-Librarian of the Gulbenkian Library.

Making use of his skill in accountancy he is also employed in the Finance Office of the Armenian Patriarchate of Jerusalem.

Sahag now teaches liturgical music and mathematics at the Patriarchate's Theological Seminary. He and his wife have no children.

Sahag Kalaydjian
The Armenian Patriarchate
Jerusalem
11th November 1984

Editor's note:

There is considerable density of implied content in this short piece. I thought the following quotation from Eusebius about traditions surrounding St. James might prove helpful:

. . . but Hegesippus, who belongs to the generation after the Apostles, gives the most accurate account of him speaking as follows in his fifth book: "The charge of the Church passed to James the brother of the Lord, together with the Apostles. He was called the 'Just' by all men from the Lord's time to ours, since many are called James, but he was holy from his mother's womb. He drank no wine or strong drink, nor did he eat flesh; no razor went upon his head; he did not anoint himself with oil, and he did not go to the baths. He alone was allowed to enter into the sanctuary, for he did not wear wool but linen, and he used to enter alone into the temple and be found kneeling and praying for forgiveness for the people, so that his knees grew hard like a camel's because of his constant worship of God. So from his great piety he was called the Just and Oblias, that is Justice and the Rampart of the people; as the prophets declare concerning him.

Ecclesiastical History II 23.

BEYOND ABSOLUTIST IDEOLOGIES: RELIGIOUS REFLECTIONS ON THE MIDDLE EAST
Colin Williams

At the time when Ayatollah Khomeini was bursting on to the international scene, leading a Shi-ite Muslim rebellion to overthrow the Shah, a prominent political figure in this country said to me in some exasperation: "I thought the time was over when religious fanatics could play a dominant role in international politics."

He should have known better—of course.

This is a time when the religious dimension has again assumed a key role—for good, or ill—even in the "secular" West, as the role of the churches in the anti-nuclear movement reminds us.

When one looks at the Middle East, perhaps the dominant issue is the rise of various forms of fundamentalism—that is, religious movements driven by the deep fears and insecurities of our time to search for meaning and identity in a return to the old religious absolutes, absolutes which are believed to transcend the flow of time.

This phenomenon is obvious in Iran, where Khomeini has centered his revolution on the restoration of the Koran and of traditional Muslim law as the sole rule of faith and practice.

Islamic fundamentalism is not only evident in this Shi-ite version, it is also powerful in Egypt in the Muslim Brotherhood, as we witnessed in the death of Sadat. In Saudi Arabia it is also evident, not least in such official pronouncements as the "Jihad," or Holy War, against Israel to fulfill their religious responsibility to restore Jerusalem to Allah. Such a pronouncement reflects the traditional belief that once the flag of Allah is planted over a territory, his followers are duly bound to defend his honor should that territory be seized by non-believers. How much more, then, is this demanded when the territory at stake is the third of the three holy cities—of which the Saudi regime sees itself as guardian.

It is precisely the strength of these movements which leads to one of the most distressing aspects of the present Middle East struggles.

It seems, at times, as though we are condemned to an intractable conflict between contradictory absolutes espoused by the warring children of Abraham.

In case we are tempted to think this is only a problem of competing Jewish and Muslim fundamentalisms, it is well to remember the strength of Christian fundamentalism in this country and the attitude of many of its leaders to Israel.

Pat Robertson of the *700 Club* TV program recently gave us his interpretation of Biblical prophecy, in which the creation of the state of Israel is seen as the promised "Return" of the "Last Days" in preparation for the final battle between people of God and the forces of the anti-Christ.

A little-noticed story from Washington at the time of the dispute over AWACs for Saudi Arabia follows this same interpretation. On October 28, 1983, this little note appeared in the New York Times:

SCRIPTURE LESSON
Senator Howard Heflin, Democrat of Alabama to reporters, after a discussion with President Reagan. . . "We got off into the Bible a little bit. We were talking about the fact that the Middle East according to the Bible, would be the place where Armageddon would start. The President was talking to me about the Scriptures and I was talking to him a little bit about the Scriptures. He interprets the Bible and Armageddon to mean that Russia is going to get involved in it."

The significance of all this for the Middle East is grasped when we realize that these various fundamentalisms are leading now, as they have in the past, to inevitable conflict.

If Israel insists that Jerusalem is, by divine right, the eternal capital of Israel, immediately Saudi Arabia, as the guardian of Islam's holy cities—Mecca, Medina and Jerusalem—feels compelled to announce a Jihad, which cannot be relaxed until Allah's sovereignty is once more restored over Jerusalem.

If Israel keeps saying that the West Bank is Judea and Samaria, which is, by divine right, the patrimony of the Jewish tribes never to be returned to Arab sovereignty, in response, Islamic fervor is inevitably aroused around the answering claim of the divine Palestinian right to sovereignty over the land.

Along that line of competing absolutes, no resolution is possible—only continuing holy war. At times, it looks as though fundamentalist Christians' only addition to this dilemma is to try to suggest to both Jew and Muslim that they should join them in a common crusade against the Russian anti-Christ.

The question is: can we find a way to transcend the old religious absolutisms? Interestingly enough, from an unwonted source, there has come a proposal which, at first sight, seems to have a strong appeal. A PLO suggestion is that what is needed in "Palestine" is a secular state in which all three—Jew, Christian, and Muslim—can live together in a pluralistic way, as they already do in the U.S. and other Western countries.

On one level, we could all say "Amen" to that. But the problem is that we must admit there is no direct road from the present hostilities in the Middle East to that situation of mutual trust. Israelis understandably see that proposal as a transparent effort to put them in a minority situation where they would be hopelessly vulnerable.

This brings us to the difficult question of the meaning of the state of Israel. Is it a religious state? In one sense, "no." Officially, it is a "secular" state—that is, a Western-type democracy with no established religion. But in another sense, "yes." It is a Jewish homeland, created as a result of the centuries of Jewish experience of seeking to live out their peculiar identity in the midst of an often hostile world.

Zionism (which created modern Israel) was largely the child of Jews who were not orthodox; hence their refusal to "establish an orthodox Jewish state." But they believed in the necessity for finding some solution to their terrible vulnerability through the re-creation of a Jewish homeland. In the period of British Mandate in Palestine, this struggle for their own territory came to a climax—leading first to the Balfour Declaration and then to the flow of Jews to the Holy Land during the Hitler period—but with the sad result that the Arabs saw it as a threat to their homeland. This led, in 1947, to the troubled U.N. realization that a partition was inevitable; and in 1948, first to war, and then to a reluctant acceptance of partition in an uneasy truce which has continued to today—punctuated by serious outbreaks of conflict, particularly at the time of the Suez Crisis of 1956, the Six Day War of 1967, and the 1973 Yom Kippur War.

Now the issue is the right of Israel to exist as a separate state (still resisted by most of the Arabs, though now accepted by Egypt and Jordan, and a little less directly by Saudi Arabia), and along with that, the right of the Palestinians to control their own homeland. Both are implied in U.N. Resolution 242 and in the Camp David Accords, but the latter has not been recognized by the influential fundamentalist right wing who say that the West Bank—Judea and Samaria—belong, by divine right, to Israel.

But that brings us back to the central point: that if one begins from the position of the competing fundamentalisms, the only way to a resolution is a fight to the finish—a holy war to settle the battle of contrary absolutes. So the question is: can this approach be transcended?

That the problem is desperately difficult, there is no point in denying; but that there must be some hope of escape from these absolutes, also seems evident.

For example, King Fahd, deviating somewhat from the aggressive anti-Zionist declaration of Jihad proclaimed by King Khalid, announced his eight-point peace plan. The Begin government quickly rejected it, because it clearly challenged Israel's claim to sole sovereignty over Jerusalem. Also, at the succeeding Arab summit, the other Arab states refused to follow Prince Fahd's approach—and yet,we should not underestimate the significance of this approach. For in it, the Saudis moved away from the old absolutist position toward the possibility of negotiation and compromise. Surely, wisdom requires that we look for any opportunity to break through the conflict of opposing absolutes towards the goal of accommodation. Inevitably, then, the spotlight turns to Israel and the question of her flexibility. There is no doubt that at present, in Israel, the religious right wing seems to be ascendant. But we should not, I believe, be misled by that. They are highly vocal, particularly on the West Bank. And yet, their appeal to the wider population in Israel is not their use of fundamentalist theology. Only a minority in Israel share that their appeal lies in their relentless vigor in insisting on Israel's right to exist against all threats, and in the insistence that they can rely on no one but themselves to fight for their survival against the continuing threat symbolized by the PLO or the Syrians, or the Arab world in general. But while this determination to fight for their own existence—no matter what the odds—is a powerful force in Israeli life, there is another mood. A mood of doubt has emerged over what has happened to Israel since 1967 and, particularly, since the war in Lebanon in 1982.

It was from an Israeli professor that I first heard the phrase "loss of innocence" applied to Israel—associated in his mind to Israel's remarkable victory in the six-day war of 1967. Before then, Israel was a political infant—a new state created in 1948, struggling for recognition and still living under the threat of ultimate extinction represented by the Holocaust.

For 19 years, Israel was the underdog, battling against the odds of history. But in 1967, Israel suddenly became old. By her sudden victory she became the military super-power of the area, and by her occupation of the West Bank-Gaza she joined the ranks of the colonial powers.

From the beginning, there was one small group in Israel represented, for example, by the ultra-orthodox religious community—"Neturei Karta"—who protested the transformation of Israel into a modern state, insisting that only with the coming of the Messiah will the Jewish state be restored. Quoting the prophetic warning to Israel to resist the temptation to become like the nations—or a state sustained by worldly power-striving to beat the world at its own game—instead of being a covenant community sustained by God's promises, they blame the government of Israel for creating friction between Israelis and Arabs by their terrritorial claims.

This group, of course, is only a tiny minority; but far more numerous are those who believe that Israel cannot be a healthy society again until she finds a way to give back the West Bank and Gaza. These Israelis are worried by the apparent policy of permanent possession that has been developed by the present government, and by the moral effect of being an occupying power.

As long as the Labor government was in office this was certainly not Israel's stated policy. Unlike the Arab states, Israel accepted U.N. Resolution 242, which sought a resolution through Israel's return of the territories gained in 1967, in exchange for recognition and the guarantee of secure borders. Whether the Labor government did all that it could to promote 242 by showing its willingness to return the West Bank in exchange for recognition, is still disputed. But with the coming of the Begin government, the Arab-Israeli relationship underwent a radical change—for better and for worse.

For better—on the border between Israel and Egypt. The Sadat initiative in 1977 resulted in Israel fully living up to the demands of 242. Israel returned Sinai and, in exchange, gained recognition from the largest Arab state.

For worse—on the boundaries with Jordan, Syria and Lebanon. The Camp David Accords might have led to progress but, as the Arabs saw it, Begin's narrow interpretation of "autonomy" for the Palestinians in the occupied territories was nothing but a transparent cover for a policy of "creeping annexation."

Shamir inherited much of Begin's support and continued his hard-line policies on the West Bank, Gaza and Lebanon. But he also experienced increasing doubts concerning the ultimate effectiveness of these policies and a rising concern that continuing occupation of the territories would, in the long run, prove disastrous for Israel—both demographically and morally.

Demographically, according to some estimates, the higher Arab birthrate could lead, by the end of the century, to more Arabs than Jews in this larger Israel. Israel would then face a choice: whether to remain a democracy and cease to be a Jewish state; or to remain a Jewish state by introducing a system of apartheid, or by driving the Arabs from the territory.

How important this concern was in Shamir's loss of mandate in the recent election, is not clear. But the present unity government represents a pause in Israel's identity struggle, not a resolution. Israel is caught between contradictory moods, unable to decide. In this, Israel matches the situation in the Arab world. And in both, at present, the stalemate between hard-line absolutists and uneasy pragmatists all too often leaves control in the hands of the absolutists. Absolutists—both Jewish and Muslim—dress their unbending insistence on their sole right to the holy land in the language of Biblical and Koranic literalism. For them, pragmatic considerations are irrelevent in the face of the absolute claim which must be enforced, if necessary, by a holy war. The pragmatists, both Israeli and Arab, are not driven by an equal fervor. Aware of the disaster that is the only end if control of events is left in the hands of the absolutists, they seek to win support by basing their argument on these rationally argued pragmatic considerations.

Is this enough to turn the tide toward accommodation—toward mutual recognition and political compromise? Probably not, for absolutists are not convinced by rational argument and, sure in the rightness of their cause, are prepared to put their belief to the test of the ultimate confrontation—Jihad or Holy War. The "true believers"—the fundamentalists—are a minority; but in the atmosphere of hate and suspicion, their fervor appeals to many a confused waverer who fears that the road of the pragmatist leads only to surrender to the absolutists of the enemy cause. The question is: can waverers be won to the side of sought conciliation?

Is there a way out? Perhaps there is. Perhaps the arguments of the pragmatists—that pursuit of rival absolutisms inevitably leads to common destruction—can be linked to a religious perception. That perception is that with all our religious conflicts, the warring children of Abraham, Jewish, Christian and Muslim share a religious heritage that is far deeper than our differences. That universal heritage should lead us to an attitude of openness in search for common ground, in the knowldege that God's truth is greater than the limited perceptions of any of us. Our common heritage assures us that God's mercy reaches out beyond our fears, suspicions, hatreds, seeking to bring the divided children of Abraham into the unity of His one family. That religious insight, matched by the empirical evidence that only this way leads to life, points us to the difficult, but necessary, path of religious dialogue. Political accommodation is needed, but it will prove fruitful only when driven by the religious conviction that we are under the divine mandate to acknowledge our common membership in the family of God.

Colin Williams

DESERT MONKS-
EUROPEAN BEDOUINS

Dan Rabinowitz

By mid-summer, the greeting ceremonies upon my frequent visits to Saleh's home were eased. One cannot remain at arm's length with a neighbor for too long, and I had become a nigh-regular dinner guest with old Saleh's family. Most evenings after dark I would ascend from the stone hut I occupied that summer, and join them at their seasonal dwelling on the granite slope.

We were the only inhabitants of the remote creek in the mountains of Sinai that summer of 1979, a good day's climb from the valley of E-Raba near the ancient monastery of Santa Caterina. The bulk of Saleh's Jebaliya Bedouin tribe live in that lower valley of E-Raba, a place which to the foreigner often seems to be at the very end of the earth. From Saleh's creek, though, twelve hundred feet above it, the lower valley now seemed tame, even placidly civilized.

That evening, I noted for the first time in greeting, how the cautious murmurs of acknowledgement were replaced by a clearer, more direct discourse. The sudden shift added a sense of time elapsing, of an intimacy crystallizing, and it gave me courage. "Saleh," I turned to the old man, seeking the familar keeness of his eyes, "what will you Jebaliya do if the Egyptian government, when it takes over from us Israelis here in three months, decides—for whatever reason—to move the monastery away, to Cairo or to Crete, or to wherever it decides to send these monks? What will become of you?"

The old man frowned at first, then lightly laughed, tossing the far-fetched prospect about his mind. Then he caught my eye, only to realize I was expecting a real reply to the question. He sat up, and his face expressed his seriousness. Slowly he began to speak, and with startling vigour and determination he exclaimed, "No one can ever move the monastery from Sinai, and leave we Jebaliya behind! The tie between us and the monks cannot be broken. If they go—then so must we." He paused a while, gazing at the fire, and then continued softly, as though twisting a piece of silk through his palm. "We are, and always will be, the children of the monastery: 'Awlad e-Deir.' We are different from all the tribes of Sinai, and our Muslim faith does not come into this at all. If we are, God forbid, torn of our land, so also will be the monks; it's not for anyone to change or question. We are the children of the monastery."

The human quest for continuity is limitless, and history often breeds the incredible, certainly in the desert. Saleh's loyalty to the twelve members of the monastic community is rooted in sixty generations of daily intercourse between the monks and the Jebaliya Bedouin. The tested reality that the two communities have a common heritage and an ongoing relationship is at the heart of old Saleh's explanation of the world and of its basic order.

In the sixth-century, about 300 years after the first persecuted Christians had begun trickling from Egypt into the wilderness of Sinai to form tiny communities of hermits in the mountains, new winds were blowing in the Middle East. The rulers of Byzantium, by then devout Christians, regarded the pioneering monks with adoration, and saw them as envoys of the theocratic empire to "the desert of the Exodus." The monastic movement thus became a political asset, and Constantinople duly rewarded the monks for their loyalty. When the monks of Sinai requested Justinian to build them a proper residence, the emperor was forthcoming. He built the monastery of the Burning Bush near mount Sinai—a huge granite structure. It was later renamed Santa Caterina. In a land where man-made structures are never larger than the length of a palm-tree trunk, and their walls no heavier than camel's hair, the monastery's massive features are astounding, indeed it changed the history of the peninsula.

In the sixth-century, however, nobody—not even the mightiest emperor on earth—could vouch for anyone's safety in the wilderness of Sinai. No matter how thick the monastery's walls were, they still stood some 1500 miles across sea and desert from Constantinople. A defence force had to be recruited. By Imperial command, two hundred families were brought to Sinai; half of them from the Balkans, and the other half from Egypt. A new community was born and the story of the Jebaliya tribe,the eternal friends of the monks began.

Back in his mountain shack old Saleh recalled the day his forefathers arrived in Sinai, a millenium and a half ago: "All the monks came out that day to meet the new people and make them welcome. They poured out of the monastery and down from their caves in the mountains. The archbishop was wearing his most majestic vestments: silk and silver robes, and a golden cross the size of a sheep's head on his chest."

Old men, when talking to the young, have the capacity to convey tales of distant days as if they had been there themselves. I was completely taken by the story. Leaning forward he picked a red hot twig from the hearth to light his hand-rolled cigarette, eyeing me sideways as if trying to see the nature of my curiosity. The white paper caught and flared, then for a moment it seemed the flame itself had been inhaled and swallowed. "There were these two lines of people in the valley, you see, nearing each other slowly. The monks were coming down from the east, and our ancestors were ascending toward the east. They met solemnly about half way. You know the place—it's near the old Carob-bread tree, the one still there as you come near the monastery. It is there where the monks and those newly come to the desert vowed eternal loyalty and signed a treaty which will never be undone. The scroll is still kept in the monastery. They have it stored with all the treasures."

Immersed in the saga, Saleh was nourished by timelessness. It is in such circumstance as legend, prayer or meditation that all of us, both old and young, seek the changeless. Saleh spoke deep into the night about an extraordinary past, but also he was sketching scenes of life in places and times much like his. He mentioned Harazin, near the monastery, the spot allotted by the monks to the newcomers and where Jebaliya still live. He described in detail the struggle for survival undertaken by the Europeans who, by Imperial decree, had been transformed into Bedouin, obliged to master herding, desert agriculture and the supply of services for pilgrims to the monastery. His narrative illuminated the mutual trust and respect that grew between the monks and the Bedouin. They survived through an intuitive collaboration founded on this essential trust—a trust that kept the two communities alive.

The stream of tribal memories expanded and clarified as the old man went on. Mirrored in his tale were experiences and thoughts of generations. Their oral history gives the Bedouin a grasp on their place in the world. It provides a context within which life may be percieved and contemplated. It is an art form and soothes the bad spirits of the dark. The Jebaliya cannot consider a world without the monastery.

Then there was a long silence until I heard the old man's voice again: "Why are you so keen to know?" he asked. "Will you remember these ancient stories as well as we do? Do you want them for a book? Will you teach them at schools?" Searching with hesitation for a reply, I realized that our peculiar inquisitiveness is as puzzling to him as his simple dignity is attractive to us. I did not answer and we withdrew into a silent accord, allowing ourselves the benefit of mutual observation and respectfully exploring our differences. In the desert one learns that our capacity for tolerance is, in fact, vast, if only we grant ourselves the mental and inner space it needs—the sort of space the Jebaliya and the monks of Santa Catarina have kept faith with for over fourteen hundred years.

For fourteen hundred and fifty years the monks have been there, incomprehensible, and the Jebaliya watched with a silent awe. With each generation, new robed youngsters kept arriving from lands the Bedouin could no longer place. Were new monks met on their arrival, in the early years, by Jebaliya longing for a word from the Balkans? How long was it before the immigrants lost hope of news from their old homes? a generation? a century? a millenium? How long was it before desert-born children could no longer relate to metaphors and visions that originated in Europe? When did their language change?

Hopes for answers to these questions are slim. As faint are our chances to trace the history of the tribesmen's religion. They are today devout Muslims. It is likely that they had been Christians in the Balkans. They could, of course, have been pagans—Gypsies—or even politcal rebels to Byzantine rule. The earliest records mentioning the Jebaliya were written four centuries after the "tribe" arrived in Sinai, and are, naturally, vague about this matter. Nor do they solve the other mystery: when and how did the Jebaliya convert to Islam?

It was less than a hundred years after the "tribe" arrived in Sinai when Islam spread across the Middle East. With it came immense pressure from the surrounding culture, from the Persian Gulf to West Africa. The Jebaliya, too, must have been caught up in this new religious wave. The monks of Santa Caterina, no longer enjoying Imperial support, had to conduct themselves with extreme caution. Helplessly, they watched their faithful "tribe" turning toward another faith and merging slowly with the desert and its culture.

Or did it fully? In 1816, Burckhardt, a Swiss traveller, heard an extraordinary story from the monks of Santa Caterina. One of them recalled a Christian Jebaliya woman whom, he said, died soon after he arrived at the monastery as a novice around the year 1750.

In 1979, looking at Saleh, I was struck by his broad, slightly Germanic features, the Roman nose and the light brown skin. Could this be the great-great grandson of Christian Jebaliya, people who had retained their "foreign" faith twelve hundred years? Or was the woman just an extraordinary conversion into Christianity, or just a wishful thought of an old monk dying thousands of miles from home?

No, even Saleh could give no answer. But things he said shed light on the fluidity and softness of boundaries between religious denominations in the desert. Here the monks and Bedouin are as free of religio-politics as they are distant from the centers of civilization. Their isolated existence in proximity to one another breeds an easy diffusion of ideas, beliefs, and myths between the two communities; a diffusion that marks the Bedouin's perception of the world.

"Rain," said Saleh, "is God's blessing to the world. We cannot understand what makes it come or stop—this knowledge is for God alone. The monks though, know. They are men of God, and what is more—they write." Literacy, for us a basic tool of daily life, is for the Bedouin a skill defying the laws of time and space. If you can perform this miracle—why shouldn't you be able to control the elements?

The Sinai Bedouin believe you can, and have believed this for at least two centuries. Burckhardt, for example, was told by his Bedouin escorts that he must not take notes of what he saw. Consequently he took to writing in secret. Once he was surprised during this sly act. His Bedouin guide, shocked by his behavior, declared that he could no longer trust the tourist: "You are spying on our land, the mountains, the grazing pastures, and on the rain that comes from the sky." Trying to calm him, Burckhardt said it was only prayers that he was writing, prayers to protect them from robbers, to which the Bedouin answered: "You might be telling the truth, but since a group of foreigners visited here some years ago and made notes of everything, rain has become scarce."

Burckhardt goes on to describe the awe with which the Bedouin regarded the monks' control over the elements. Following one destructive flood, a Bedouin came to the monastery in outrage, claiming the monks were responsible for the damage: ". . . you opened the book too much and now we are all drowning."

In 1841, Robinson, another visitor to Sinai, was told by the monks that a few years earlier a Bedouin sheikh was spreading the rumor that the monks were responsible for the three-year drought then afflicting the Sinai. The sheikh finally announced to the archbishop that unless the monks were to immediately climb the holy mount of Sinai and pray for rain he would harm the monastery. They did as commanded.

Elsewhere Robinson tells how his guide, Bishara, begged him to persuade the monks to allow them to open the window facing south in the chapel atop Mt. Sinai. This, the Bedouin explained, would bring about the right "connection," and rain would come. "Yes, God has the final say," he admitted, ". . . but the monks have the prayer book that can persuade Him."

Palmer, who visited Sinai in the 1860s, relates a Bedouin legend according to which, Moses, who etched his book into the rock of Mt. Sinai, originally made rain to fall at fixed intervals of forty days and nights. The monks later brought the book into the monastery and built it into the walls of the Chapel of The Burning Bush. When they want rain—they have to open the window and say the potent words.

Saleh is, likewise, certain that the monks do indeed possess this power. "Once, not long ago," he said, "there was a drought, and this Bedouin was entrusted by the monks with an important mission. He was to put a parchment inscribed with the secret divine prayer for rain at the upper end of a valley where many of the monastery's orchards were. Seeking his own good, he betrayed the monks and placed the parchment at the upper reach of a valley where his family's orchards were. Rain came on the valley where the parchment was hidden. But instead of blessings, the rain brought a curse: the valley flooded with run off and the man's orchards were all washed away. You cannot cheat God, now, can you?"

Rain, life's vital liquid, is often closely related to life's vital substance, bread; and in Jebaliya tradition, both are associated with the monastery. For centuries, in fact, until the 1960s , the monastery served the tribe as its primary source of subsistence, and its only reliable one. The daily distributions of loaves at the monastery wall have been an indispensable institution of their life all along.

Three times a week at dusk two Jebaliya would arrive at the monastery, collect some 500 pounds of flour from the quartermaster, and set to work. By midnight, huge piles of dough would be at hand and the baking got under way. By morning, hundreds of rolls, each a man's palm size were ready, available for distribution. By mid-morning, the daily Jegaliya congregation-from thirty to a hundred—would have assembled at the foot of the northern wall where the chief monk, assisted and advised by one of the veteran Bedouin servants of the monastery, would then begin the distribution. No Jebaliya man was to exceed the quota of five loaves at a time. No woman was to get more than four, unless she was with child—a fact the veteran at the top of the wall had to affirm. Children got three loaves and babies, two.

The story goes that in the 1950s, young Jebaliya girls used to play this witty trick on the elderly monks: They would fold a piece of cloth to an elongated bundle and carry it in their arms as it it were a child in order to get an extra loaf. The monks, good sports, would go along for awhile and then putting on an angry face chase the ten year old "mothers" away.

But rain and bread are not the only gifts God sends through the faithful monks. Fertility and health, riches and tranquillity, cannot prevail without God's "Baraka" (blessing) with which the men of the monastery are well endowed. It is this celestial blessing, the Bedouin told Palmer in 1868, that renders evil thoughts directed at the monks quite harmless, and also it is this very blessing that the Jebaliya seek on their annual summer pilgrimage to the monastery.

The old man sighed, "The pilgrimmage to Santa Caterina was the biggest day in our calandar. The whole tribe would arrive—young and old, weak or strong, rich or poor. Even the women came along, and the gathering took place at the holy shrine of Nabi Haroun within eyesight of the monastery. It was like a real migration. Campsites vanished overnight all over the territory and suddenly a whole city of tents appeared out of nothing near the monastery.

Farhana, Saleh's wife, now joined us. She was a lean, fragile figure, her black eyes sparkling in the tiny space between the face cover and a bundle of hair stuck, Jebaliya style, firmly on her forehead. "What is it you are talking about?" she asked as she settled on the blanket by the fire. "The Zawarah of old," Saleh answered. She made a faint trilling sound and gazed into the softly glowing hearth as if she could follow her eyes through the fire and into her past. Her voice echoed, it seemed, like distant memories of hollering down empty wells. "For us women, the pilgrimage was a treat, a real dream. So many tents, rows on rows of them, so many people talking, milling around, walking and gossiping and riding camels. We cooked and ate and danced and sang our songs, and for weeks after we went on laughing on the strength of each hour of gossip. I would get to see my father's family who would ride up all the way from the plains. A real feast . . ."

On occasions such as the tribal gathering, the Bedouin community becomes a profoundly tangible one, an organic entity far more than the sum of its parts. Underlying the routines lies a complex lattice of social relationships, a hierarchy of power and of wealth, of status and prestige. Every gesture, every sound and facial expression, counts.

The first two days of the Jebaliya pilgrimage were given to the business of reunions and news and vital inter-clan dynamics, helped along by much bitter coffee followed by thick sweet tea. The third day brings a change in direction. The focus changes from the internal tribal scene to the monastery at the head of the valley. Farhana began to build up a world of images: "Right after breakfast, the procession would begin up to the monastery. We left the tents behind at Nabi Haroun and the whole tribe marched up, all of us wearing our finest clothes and headgear. You know the fork near the monastery garden—there we take the southern path circling the walls on the Mt. Sinai side. When we got to the foot of the northern wall, there, where by noon is some shade, everybody rested. The whole procession waited there until the men were called inside the walls to visit the chapel." Saleh picked up the tale about how the men were invited into the monastery to visit the Chapel of The Burning Bush: "They used to take us in as small groups. First we went into the chapel and slowly walked up to its end to touch the silver coffin of the Saint Gatrina. Our elders say she was the daughter of Moses, and we were allowed to touch the relief of her body all carved in silver. On the way out of the chapel we passed the place that was special for Moses, and prayed there. All ancient kings and saints are holy."

Farhana was now busy preparing some more tea. Her head and body moved surely, steadily, while her fingers nimbly searched and found and fitted. Quickly she placed the right amount of dry twigs on the dying fire, then softly blew at it , leaning forward as if attempting to seduce it. The sparkle caught and now the fire was crackling again. Soon the kettle was steaming and it was time to taste the tea. Holding the "Burga" (face cover) with her left hand, Farhana swiftly moved her right, holding the tiny cup, under the cloth. Eyes down, cautiously she sipped the boiling liquid. Satisfied with the taste and strength, she now poured for us. "We women," she said, handing a cup across to Saleh, "were not invited into the monastery. Instead, we stood at the foot of the wall, chanting. There was a song for Moses and one for Gatrina: . . .O Moses, O Gatrina, our masters and protectors . . . we wish for your benevolence; each year we come on pilgrimage to you . . . Then, as we were singing there, a special give-away of bread took place. The monk in charge of food came out and threw two loaves of bread for each person. Not just tiny rolls like every day—big, chunky loaves especially baked for this day." The men would now come out to rejoin the women and prepare for the climax of the day. And suddenly, there it was. The monks, led by the Archbishop, appeared at the top of the wall wearing silk to look down at the tribal gathering. The monotonous hum from down below now gradually became an enthusiastic chant, a rhythmic hymn. There stood the desert people, their faces lifted, conveying their songs of praise to God through an enigmatic present in Sinai: the ancient kings and saints of early days present in the mythic songs, and the living mediators arrayed on the wall in their black robes."

We sipped the tea in silence for a while. Then I asked a question I soon realized the old man could not quite answer: "Why have the Jebaliya ceased to go on this pilgrimage after 1966, and not yet renewed it?" Saleh was taken aback. He muttered, "I don't really know...there was some dispute, I remember, about who was to purchase the she-camel for the 1967 event . . . and then we decided not to hold the gathering that year. Then later . . . people, I hear, could not come to pligrimage because everyone was busy with work after the Israeli occupation started. People went away to Eilat and the coast to work and save some money, and had not free time. That's how it came to be, I think . . . I wish it hadn't."

I sat there thinking of the real reasons. The reluctance of both communities to openly state their mutual loyalty in the presence of a third party—be it Israel from 1967 onwards, or Egypt now. And there was the declining economic significance of the monastery which took away some of its meaning in Jebaliya symbolism. I thought of the new generation of Jebaliya, youngsters for whom the monastery is merely a physical entity, a place where the tourists come. But then I looked at Saleh, again and theorising gave way to concrete remembrance. Suddenly, I saw his image as I recalled it in the monastery's courtyard three months previously when he attended the smaller, less overt Easter gathering. The monks were standing there together, smiling and handing bunches of coloured Easter eggs and dates to Jebaliya tribesmen. The line of waiting Bedouin gradually shortened, and as Saleh approached his gaze was fixed on the Archbishop, his employer and partner since the 1930s. His turn arrived and the Archibishop leaned forward, stretched his hand into the basket, and placed a red egg and a green one in the old man's opened palm. Their eyes met momentarily with a spark of mutual respect. For Saleh, the black-robed man was not some esoteric foreigner who somehow had wandered into the Sinai. For him, the Archbishop was a part of the ancestral domain, an indispensable feature of the only order in this ever-changing world, a living banner of continuity.

I must have fallen asleep after the stories. The early morning chill woke me to the discovery that there was a blanket over me. Saleh and Farhana must have slipped it over me to keep the cold away. I lay awake there for a while, surrounded by the total silence of the desert night maturing to dawn. Then, there was a stir at Saleh's sleeping quarters, soon after which I saw the old man's lean silhouette moving across the faint blue sky toward the orchard in the valley. I watched him climb slowly across the garden wall like a custodian dutifully entering a shrine. A wooden gate, held loosely by pins of crooked metal, squeaked, and the slight figure disappeared into the dark. There among the pear and almond trees, the apples, peaches, grapes, and plums which were first imported to Sinai by the monks fifteen hundred years ago, there is Saleh's place. He loves those trees as his ancestors did, natives of southern Europe, as the newly born loves his mother's heart beat. They make his element.

My last summer in Sinai was soon over. Egypt was gradually assuming sovereignty over the Sinai again, and Santa Caterina was scheduled to be handed over by November. Staying became out of the question for an Israeli. Autumn found me making my first steps through London's academia.

The last time I saw Saleh, in 1981, we were both far from our element. Academic work brought me to Cairo. The hospitality and warmth of the inhabitants could only partly dismiss the profound disorientation I felt. I was alone in what, for decades, used to be the heart of hatred and fear of my country.

One day I took a taxi to an institute about which I had often heard from friends among the Jebaliya—the monastery's property and its residence in Cairo. I had heard that the place used to be a haven in the old days for tribesmen visiting the teeming city. As I walked through the iron gate into the lush greenery and silence of the European enclave behind the walls, the last thing I anticipated was to meet a Jebaliya. The idea of Sinai Bedouin taking refuge and finding assistance there was, for me, a distant fantasy of days bygone, a phenomenon alluded to by nineteenth-century travellers and pilgrims in their travel-books (normally in the section devoted to preparations in Cairo before departure to the desert.) So, when the doorman said something about an old Bedouin who had arrived from Sinai at the monastery's expense for eye treatment some weeks before, and who was staying in a flat owned by the monks just around the corner, I could not resist and asked to see the man.

Bemused, the doorman consented to show me to the flat. The building was evidently very old. The stairs, although just firm enough to hold our weight, had no railing, and the safest way was to keep as close to the wall as possible. Curious eyes watched from neighboring flats as we climbed to the third floor and into a dark, poorly ventilated place. Blindfolded, lying on a mat, there was Saleh! Choking, I came near to the old man. Startled by an approaching body, he sat up to greet the unknown visitor. I was truly beside myself with joy! I experienced the intensity of the scene and, at the same time, watched as in a distant dream. Right in front of me, alone, in a city larger than a Bedouin can hope to comprehend, was my friend from wadi Jibal. The monks did not forsake a servant in need.

The extraordinary nature of our meeting, 300 miles away from Saleh's home, astonishingly, did not strike him as odd at all. Showing no surprise, the old man simply expressed great delight at the reunion. Within moments, we were in the business of desert chit-chat, gossip, and the exchange of information as though we had never stopped. For a sweet last time, just shortly before my old friend's exit, we let our memories carry us to our beloved mountain.

Dan Rabinowitz
Tel Aviv, Israel

THE CARMELITE STORY

"Once Upon A Time There Was A Mountain"

Mother Tessa Bielecki and
Father William McNamara, O.C.D.

The truth is much too large and inscrutable to be contained inside neat, tidy, categorical concepts and ideas. Doctrine and theology are indispensable, but they are not enough. The Christian faith did not initially come to us as systematic theology; it came as story. The story faded and monumental doctrinal theses developed. In losing the story, we lose both the power and the glory. We have committed the unpardonable sin of transforming an exciting story into a dull system. We must recover the story if we are to recover a faith for our day. We must tell and retell the old story and, in the telling of it, discover and discern our own story.

The Carmelite story begins with Mt.Carmel rising directly out of the blue waters of the Mediterranean Sea. Carmel begins abruptly at the water's edge, climbs rapidly to a height of 1800 feet and then joins a range of hills hugging the coastline for twenty-one miles to a point where the narrow shore widens into the Plain of Sharon. The mountain runs in a northwesterly direction from Megiddo towards the Mediterranean and then thrusts a promontory into the sea to form the south side of the Bay of Haifa.

"Mt. Carmel: tall, massive, brooding at the water's edge. The site of innumerable Biblical scenes. The home of the fiery prophet Elijah, the mountain dwelling of Elisha and his school of prophets. The image used by Solomon in his "Song of Songs" to describe the bride's alluring beauty. The mountain retreat of early Christian monks who prayed there and lived in its caves. The scene of battle and bloodshed for marauding armies which climbed its steeps—Saracens and Turks, Crusaders and the French armies of Napoleon. Rich with history, venerable with age, confidante of a thousand stories of personal human drama. Part mountain, part symbol it stands in the new Israeli State, evocative of the past, but an enduring and tangible testimony that the spirit of the great realities enacted there, Judaic and Christian, will never die or be lost."[1]

Mt. Carmel is the "homeland of the heart" for the Carmelite family, those who live and breathe the spirituality that grows out of the physicality of that mountain. In every century, Carmelites everywhere need to breathe the air of the heights of Carmel if they are to live. Carmelites are mountain men and women, called to match the mountain that gives them their name. The stellar moments of human excellence are celebrated by mountain men and women who climb to the pinnacles of passion, the mountain tops, and are transfigured there. There are many such mountains in human history. Some are famous: Sinai, Horeb, Tabor, Calvary, Carmel. The men and women who scale these mountains and enjoy such peak human experiences are like the mountains themselves: ethereal and earthy, eerie and erotic. Erotic in the radical sense of that word, in its real and deepest meaning: a reaching and a stretching of every fiber of the whole human person for the fullness of life.

The word Carmel in Hebrew means "garden." Nicholas the Frenchman, one of the first Prior Generals of the Carmelite Order, describes the beauty of Carmel's garden. Relating to the mountain on a deeply personal level he calls its hills and slopes his "conventual brethren":

> "The mountains, according to the prophet Isaiah, surround us with great sweetness . . . These mountains, our conventual brethren . . . unite themselves with the psalms which we sing to the glory of the Creator as a lute accompanying words. While we praise the Lord, the roots grow, the grass becomes green, the branches and trees rejoice in their own fashion and applaud our praises. Wonderful flowers, delicately scented, gladden our solitude with their laughter. The silent light of the stars tells us the hours set apart for God's service. Wild growing things cover us with shade and offer us their pleasant fruits. All our sisters, the creatures who, in solitude, charm our eyes or our ears, give us rest and comfort. In silence they give forth their beauty like a song encouraging our soul to praise the wonderful Creator."[2]

As Thomas Merton notes, this love of nature is not to be called "Franciscan," "as if St. Francis had a monopoly on the contemplation of the

Creator in His creation."[3] This view is essentially Catholic, Christian, and in fact, human: our universal human heritage.

THE DESERT EXPERIENCE

The story of Carmel is not only the story of a mountain, but the story of the desert which surrounds it. The desert plays a vastly important role in Judaic, Christian, and Islamic traditions, and in the monasticism of both East and West. The desert is the place where we encounter God, the place where God visits his people. The desert is not merely a natural phenomenon, but a way of life.

The complexity of civilization vanishes in the desert. Life is reduced to simple decisions; a wrong decision may be fatal. The desert is no place for diversions, distractions, luxuries, or trivia. In the desert we rediscover the difference between essentials and non-essentials; mediocrity becomes impossible.

The desert is a challenge, an invitation to a contest: whether or not we can come to terms with the bare and undiminished facts of reality—the reality of our deluded and denatured selves, our devastated and dehumanized world, and the reality of God. We cannot master the elements of the desert, but if we hope to cope with them, we had better master ourselves.

The desert evokes our latent capacity for initiative and exploration. It interrupts the ordinary pattern of our daily existence and the stultifying process of our conventional routine piety. It disengages us from our regular round of respectable human activities. We learn to be still, alert, perceptive and recollected, so that issues become clear and reality becomes recognizable and un-ambiguous. We see real things, not mere shadows. We experience real events, not merely a succession of pseudo-events. We know ourselves, not merely projected images of ourselves. We know God, not abstractions about God—not even the theology of God, but the much more mysterious God of theology: the God of Abraham, Moses, Elijah, John the Baptist, Peter and Paul, the Fathers of the desert; the Allah of Mohammed . . . the God of saints and the God of sinners.

The only way to God is the way of the real. The desert shatters our managerial complacency, our spiritual torpor, our barren and bloodless dalliance with the pretty poisons of life, and forces us into confrontation with the real. The central pervading atmosphere of the desert is death. But it is not all that bleak. The beauty of the desert is spectacular! The life you find there in tenacious trees, blooming cactus, and hardy wild flowers, is as startling as the death you find in dry creek beds, blowing "dust-devils," and sunbleached bones.

The desert experience is not all darkness and dread, but light and joy in the Lord who is sheer delight. The manifestation of God's glory is an indispensable element in the desert experience. YHVH did not call his people out of Egypt and into the desert for nothing, nada, but for nothing but God, the All, toda y nada; to live fully and exuberantly in the divine mileau of the Promised Land.

The desert is a long arduous trek through purgation into Paradise. The experience begins with the free, deliberate decision to suffer. It ends with the uproariously happy surprise of being in harmony with the universe, in the glory of God's presence, and incalculably in love with all that is.[4]

The spirituality of the Carmelite tradition reflects the spirit of the desert: immediate, essential, uncompromising. That means no formulas, no methods, no techniques. "What would men (and women), fiercely devoted to spiritual liberty and accustomed to the breeze that comes from the desert, have to do with special forms and complicated methods? Instinctively they cling to what is most simple and ordinary because that is what makes it possible for them to give themselves in peace to the one thing necessary."[5] Carmelites are notoriously anti-technique. They offer freedom and simplicity to our contemporary culture where even the realm of prayer is spoiled by technology.

ELIJAH AND OUR LADY OF MT. CARMEL

The Arabs call Mt. Carmel, Mt. Saint Elijah. Elijah, the prophet, is the moral founder of the Carmelite tradition, the spiritual father, the masculine archetype in whom every Carmelite sees themself as in a mirror. The spirit of Elijah is a "double spirit" of contemplation and action.

Elijah appears abruptly in Jewish history. The Bible gives us no preliminary information about him. We first meet him in the First Book of Kings through a bold declaration: "Behold the living God in whose presence I stand." (1 Kings 17:1). These words comprise the shortest and most effective autobiography ever written. They have remained the charter of all contemplatives ever since, and particularly the Carmelite family.

Elijah's statement says nothing about his personal background and points instead to the reality of God. The primary fact of Elijah's existence is that "the Lord God lives." This shows us that the contemplative must be God- conscious and not self-conscious. Thomas Merton calls Elijah's proclamation an "allegory of the whole Carmelite vocation."

Forty days and forty nights Elijah walked into the desert to find God where he had first revealed himself to Israel. There in eremitical solitude, Elijah became a God-intoxicated man and a prominent, crucial figure in the most pressing and dramatic issues of his day. He resolved the problems of the Jews with desert directness. Fearlessly facing a full assembly of his countrymen on Mt. Carmel, he lashed out at their indecision with the stringent words: " How long, O Israel, will you limp between two sides? If the Lord be God, follow him! But if Baal, then follow him." (1 Kings 18:21) He then challenged the priests of Baal to a showdown of strength, a trial by fire.

Ahab, King of Israel at the time of Elijah, called him "the man who gives Israel no rest," or, "troubler of Israel." If the Elijan spirit is a double spirit then that spirit is double trouble! Elijah is a figure of absolutely primeval force, a wild unstemmable colossus of God, a gnat on the rump of society.

The Mother of Carmel is Our Lady of Mt. Carmel: Mary, the Mother of Jesus. Carmel lives and breathes Mary because she represents another ideal and provides crucial feminine balance to the fierce Elijan spirit.

At the end of the Old Testament, Mary, the woman wrapped in silence, emerges with incomparable feminine force. Hundreds and thousands of years of stammering quest are concentrated and burst forth in this valiant Virgin's fiat: "Be it done according to thy word" (Lk.1:38).

According to the Christian tradition, in Mary culminates all the expectation of the Jewish people. Mary is the epitome and incarnation of the long waiting of twenty centuries. She achieved the indispensable human disposition: wise passiveness, openness, and receptivity. God prepared to come as an infant once humanity had built a cradle. Mary was the cradle, the marvelous flower sprung out of the Israelite desert.

Within the Carmelite tradition, Mary first appears in a vision to Elijah as he sat on the top of Mt. Carmel looking out over the Mediterranean Sea. Elijah sees a cloud "no larger than a man's hand," which brings with it rain in torrents over the parched land of Israel (1 Kings 18:41-46). For hundreds of years Carmelites have interpreted the cloud as Mary, a symbol of the reign of grace which Mary inaugurates by bearing Christ into the world.

The cloud has always been a significant symbol in the Judeo- Christian tradition: a sign or even a way of freedom. Moses' cloud led the Israelites out of their respectable Egyptian enslavement. In our own day all of us long to be liberated from the entanglements of the acquisitive mind, by what the famous fourteenth century mystic called "The Cloud of Unknowing." Elijah's vision of the cloud was an experiential anticipation of the freedom from Satanic forces, a freedom we would all come to enjoy in the Kingdom of Christ's love ushered in by the contemplative stillness and virtuous activity of Mary of Nazareth. The cloud, composed of air and water, is a specially apt symbol of the feminine filled with the true Sun who is Christ.

TWELFTH AND SIXTEENTH CENTURY CARMELITES

The first Carmelites in recorded history appear in 1155 A.D., living as apostolic hermits in solitude and contemplation in huts and caves atop Mt.Carmel. As Thomas Merton explains: "The first Carmelites had initiated something quite original and unique . . . neither the eremitical nor the apostolic aspects of this new life were systematically organized and neither was the subject of a formal program."[6] Eventually these men asked Albert, Patriarch of Jerusalem, to draw up a rule reflecting the way of life they had spontaneously adopted. Unlike the more formal and juridical rules of other monastic traditions, there is "nothing narrowly literal" about the Rule of St. Albert. It is more like "an invitation to live rather than a formula of life."[7]

Many of these original Carmelites had been Crusaders. Their spirituality was a rugged, manly, virile piety, the spirituality of the soldier, the fighter, the warrior. There is a virile note in every measure of the Rule of St. Albert.

Under persecution these original Carmelite hermits were forced to leave Mt.Carmel and establish foundations in Europe where they became over-organized,over-crowded, and over-active. Once they moved off the mountain and out of the desert they lost their unique and invaluable charism and ceased to make their distinct contribution to human culture.

In sixteenth-century Spain, St. Teresa of Avila and St. John of the Cross were pressed by God to restore the original, primitive Carmelite ideal. This Teresian reform added dramatic cloistered features in order to make the contemplative life possible in the distracted urban life of Europe.

Teresa of Avila was beautiful, charming and full of good humor. She played the tambourine, danced among her sisters with castanets, and prayed, "Oh God, deliver me from sour-faced saints !" One day her sisters found her in the convent kitchen relishing a roast partridge. Seeing their scandalized expressions, Teresa exclaimed, simply and passionately: "When I pray and fast . . . I pray and fast; and when I eat partridge...I eat partridge!"

Teresa was a remarkably wise and wild woman who reformed not only convents of women, but monasteries of men. Her spirit was militant as well as matrimonial. She shows us the muscular personality needed to embrace the "double spirit" of Elijah, to balance contemplation and action, work and prayer, the inner and the outer life. In her "Way of Perfection," she told her nuns: "I want you to be strong men." According to one of her own friars, "A breath of warrior energy animated her."

Like St. Teresa, his madre and mentor, St. John of the Cross considered himself a conquistador of the spiritual life. St. John, like St. Teresa, is a Mystical Doctor of the Church who outlines the Carmelite path as an arduous ascent up the slopes of Mt. Carmel. Mt. Carmel is the central symbol in John's mystical theology; not only historical but trans-historical; not merely physical but metaphysical. In John's spiritual writings, Mt.Carmel is the Mount of Perfection, a metaphor, of course, for Mt. Calvary itself, where we are all to be crucified with Christ, only then to be resurrected and made new.

THE YIN-YANG OF CARMEL

The history of the Carmelite tradition provides a fascinating study of yin-yang, the Oriental principle of feminine-masculine complementarity in the universe. The story of Carmel shows an unusual masculine-feminine balance.

We see the masculine principle in the geography of the mountain, which reaches and stretches itself out of the feminine earth into the aerie heights. Although the spirituality which grows out of the desert is rugged and virile, the geography of the desert is markedly feminine with its wide open spaciousness abandoned to the ravishments of sun and wind and rain.

Elijah is a dramatically masculine figure phallically symbolized by fire. The femininity of Our Lady of Mt. Carmel is aptly captured in the symbol of the cloud in which she "appeared" to Elijah. Although the first twelfth-century Carmelite hermits were all men, they were deeply devoted to Our Lady of Mt. Carmel, and named themselves after her. They were also radically in touch with Mother Earth, as Nicholas the Frenchman has illustrated.

In order to reform the Carmelite Order in sixteen-century Spain, St. Teresa of Avila exhibited a strong animus in her "warrior energy," but her life, letters, and mystical writings clearly reveal an utterly feminine woman complemented by her confessor and faithful friend, St. John of the Cross, a fiery new Elijah immersed in the "Living Flame of Love."

This masculine-feminine complementarity reaches its apogee in the mystery of Jesus Christ. In the Christian tradition that dimension of the

Godhead we call Wisdom (Sophia) is feminine. Feminine Wisdom unites with the masculine Jesus and the Christ emerges as the fullness of man-womanhood.

It seems natural and inevitable that the Christian spirit of Carmel which reflects such masculine-feminine balance throughout its venerable history should now be expressed in a mixed community of men and women called the Spiritual Life Institute, a small monastic community of hermits founded in 1960 with a mandate from the visionary Pope John XXIII. This new community recaptures the spirit of the mountain and the desert, of Elijah and Our Lady, of John of the Cross and Teresa, and lives according to the primitive Carmelite ideal in a contemporary manner. It is ironic, and yet a typical trait of history, that such a fitting contemporary form of contemplative life in the modern world turns out to be an ancient monastic model . . . primitive Carmelite eremiticism.

Spiritual Life Institute hermits live like the twelfth-century Carmelites who followed the example of the prophet Elijah and lived on Mt. Carmel as laymen under a common monastic rule characterized by simplicity and minimal structure to enable them to offer God a pure and undivided heart. Each one has a separate hermitage where he "meditates day and night on the law of the Lord unless engaged in some other legitimate occupation" (Rule of St. Albert).

This monastic life is a rhythm of work and play, solitude and togetherness, fast and feast, discipline and wildness, sacrifice and celebration, contemplation and action, occupational and spousal prayer. Lauds is prayed communally every morning at six, and Vespers every evening at five except on days of solitude. On Saturday evenings the community ushers in the Sabbath with Compline, Benediction, and all-night Vigil before the Blessed Sacrament.

Several hours every day, two days a week and one week of every month is spent in complete solitude. Manual labor varies with the season. Sunday is a day of holy leisure when the hermits break their ordinary pattern of existence and waste the whole day creatively by praying, playing and enjoying true Sabbath rest.

Hermitages are open for private retreats to men and women, married and unmarried, clergy and lay, to Christians, members of other traditions and those without any particular religious affiliation—people from all walks of life who feel called to go "into the desert and pray"(Mk.1:35). Retreatants participate in the monastic rhythms of the community or choose solitude in their own hermitages. The overall effort is to create a lively human atmosphere of prayer so that visitors will be more deeply and enduringly affected by a contagion of prayer rather than a program of prayer. The number of guests is limited to preserve silence and solitude which provide an indispensable climate not only for prayer but for deeper human relatedness.

The heart of this life is the desert experience. "I will espouse you, lead you into the desert, and there I will speak to your heart" (Hosea 2:14). In the Judeo-Christian Scriptures the desert, the mountain, the woods and other solitary places are used synonymously to refer to the basic wilderness experience. No one can live a fully human life without some experience of the wilderness. The desert experience is not meant to be an isolated experience, but an informative and empowering source of realistic and responsible contemplative action in society, following the examples of Elijah, Jesus, and Teresa of Avila.

Nova Nada Hermitage was founded in Kemptville, Nova Scotia, in 1972. Nada Hermitage, originally founded in 1963 in Sedona, Arizona, is being relocated in Crestone, Colorado, at the base of Kit Carson Peak, which is being renamed Mt. Carmel.

As the Spiritual Life Institute commemorates its 25th anniversary year in 1985, the men and women of the community celibate as faithful sons and daughters of the ancient Carmelite tradition, but also as pioneers, pathfinders, and pilgrims of the Absolute. We must not depend too much on the story, on the map, on what is known, safe and familiar. Dependency would kill us, for it is the unknown that gives us life. The unknown flowers when we are receptive to it and allow it to enter. The unknown carries us to the constantly forming edge of the world where light, beauty, and ecstasy are found. There is no other path to the spiritual, to the creative, to the real.

Mother Tessa Bielecki
Father William McNamara, O.C.D.
Crestone, Colorado

1. Peter-Thomas Rohrbach, O.C.D., *Journey to Carith: The Story of the Carmelite Order* (Garden City, New York: Doubleday, 1966), p.17.

2. Thomas Merton, *Disputed Questions* (New York: Farrar, Straus, and Giroux, 1953), p. 235.

3. Ibid.

4. These reflections on the desert are expanded in a chapter entitled "The Desert Experience" in *Mystical Passion* by William McNamara, O.C.D., originally published by Paulist Press in 1977. *Mystical Passion* is currently out of print but will eventually be republished by the Spiritual Life Institute, Crestone, Colorado 81131.

5. Paul Marie de la Croix, O.C.D., *"Carmelite Spirituality," Some Schools of Catholic Spirituality*, ed. Jean Gautier, p.115.

6. Merton, p.204.

7. de la Croix, pp. 123-124.

THE SHIP OF SAFETY

Sheikh Mohammed Sayad Al Jemal Al Rifai Ash-Shadhulli

بسم الله الرحمن الرحيم
الاسلام الدين الخالص

How to travel in the Ark of Noah
a ship which crosses all the seas:
an understanding of Islam in light of the aspects
of al Shariah, al Iman, al Ihsan and al Eeqan.

This is a story about a boat ride across a great sea, so great that there are within this sea—many seas. What is the nature, form and substance of the Ship of Noah which can carry one across all the waters? It is important to quickly discover the nature of this boat, to get in it and ride, because turbulent waters cover the face of the earth today as they did in the time of Noah, may Peace and Blessings be upon him and all that follow in the straightness of his Way.

The ship which can carry us through the stormy waters of this world to the opposite shore of God's Peace and Promise is surrender to the Will of God (Allah): *al Islam.* Islam is a Jewel of holy Wisdom and Mercy transmitted from the Most High through the agency of His Prophets and Messengers. Being such a Jewel from on high, it bears many facets and dimensions within it. As one surrenders more and more deeply more facets and inner dimensions of the Jewel reveal themselves; one's perception of the Ship and the water through which it passes transforms in voyage.

In the beginning, the Shariah (Law) is the chariot. It is necessary to get into this vehicle to begin to travel; but in and of itself, the exoteric Law cannot carry one across all the seas. The Law is nevertheless necessary for the protection of al Islam; it is like bark which protects the holy Tree. Without bark, the tree could not live, for the sap of its essence would run out and be lost.

The sap of the essence of the Tree is *al Iman:* Faith. It is the Faith of the Believers which keeps Islam alive in every age—and keeps the form of the Law itself vitalized from within; the sap flows throughout the tree down to its roots, giving nourishment to every part.

The Tree is rooted in Divine Insight: *al Ihsan.* As one continues to travel, the Knowledge derived from this Insight is transformed again into Illuminated Wisdom: al Eeqan, and this is the veritable life of the Tree of all the souls of the Prophets and the Faithful (Mumminin) throughout eternity. By virtue of this Illuminated Wisdom within it, the Tree is rooted in the very ground of God's Being, and it rises into the sky of His Grace, branching out in every direction as He wishes.

The holy Tree is the Ship for the Family of God. This is the vehicle in which not only Noah, but all of the Prophets and Messengers have traveled. When one begins to surrender to the Law of God, the waters through which he moves, as well as the craft he rides in, are perceived in relation to His Order in everything. As awareness of the vehicle deepens, Faith is awakened, both the Ocean and the Ship of Faith reflect his faith itself; he moves by faith through an Ocean of Faith. Then the vehicle transforms again; when Knowing is awakened by the power of faith, and then he travels through a Sea of Knowledge—knowledge being reflected back to him by all and everything that he voyages through. When this knowledge realizes the holy Light that is hidden within it, the vehicle transforms again into al Eeqan, the Illuminated Wisdom of Allah. In this Ship one can cross every sea, and reach the opposite shore. But in Truth, there is no destination for the voyager in the Ship of al Eeqan, because just as the shore is Light, so is the Ocean the Light of Allah, and the Ship and the traveller himself, all are Light, and there is no difference between one manifestation and another, because the forms are there only as a pretext. In reality, everything is of the nature of the Light of Allah, and nothing else exists.

To travel through all the stages in this voyage, we begin in the Name of Allah, the Merciful, the Compassionate, to journey in the Ship of His Law. Our holy Master, our Maulana the Prophet Muhammed, may Peace and Blessings be upon him, said, "Any person in whom Allah wishes to awaken the Good (al Kher), He makes him knowledgeable in the Din

(Religion). Allah is the Giver, while I am the divider and the distributor (al Qasim)." The nation of those in whom Allah has awakened al Kher shall be governed by the Order of Allah and the Uma, the Family of the Believers; and the Family of Allah will not be harmed by any people who deviate from the Straight Way unless the Order of Allah commands it. Whomever He wishes, He will teach him and make him understand; then this person will become knowledgeable in the Order and the Judgement and the Laws of the Din (literally: Religion manifested in behaviour and action) and the teaching of the *Holy Qur'an*. This person, to whom Allah has taught the Word of the Qur'an and the Judgement, encompasses the good of this world (dunniya) and the next (akher). "Ya Hadee Allahu li Noorihee Manyesha": Allah leads to His Light whom He will". Whomever Allah wishes to lift out of the turbulent waters of this dark world, He picks up with His own Hands and puts him in the Ship of Surrender. This is the inner meaning of the Din, Qur'an and Judgement; and if anyone is not truly prostrated before the Presence of the One who gives the Law, no matter how many injunctions he follows with his mind, he is not in Truth, a Muslim.

The literal meaning of *al Fiqh* is understanding; the traditional meaning is the knowledge of the principles and rules of the Shariah (Law, Order, Path, or literally: a way that leads to water). The word Fiqh simply means a knowledge of things, but it has come to signify the knowledge of the Din which, with insight, leads one to the essence of the Law, and raises this understanding to a higher dimension than all other sciences. A man becomes Faqiha when he embodies the Fiqh, understanding the Law and following it. Fiqh has then come to refer particularly to the knowledge of the Path: al Islam, al Iman and al Ihsan.

And it came in the Hadith of the Prophet, Peace and Blessings be upon him, as reported by Omar Ibn al Khitab, that one day a dark-haired man dressed in deep white came to the Prophet without any signs of traveling; and nobody knew that person. He came close to the Prophet and he said: "O Muhammed, inform me about *Islam*." And the Messenger of Allah said to him, "Islam is to witness: 'La illaha il Allah wa Muhmmed Rasoolillah; to practice the *Salaat* (daily prayers); to pay *Zakat* (charity); to make the *Hajj* (pilgrimage to Mecca) if you have the means; and to fast in *Ramadan*.' " And the man said to Muhammed, "You speak the Truth." The people sitting around were amazed that this person asks and affirms. The man with the dark hair and the white clothes said: "Please tell me about *al Iman*." The Prophet answered: "The faith is to believe in Allah and the Angels, Books and Messengers, to believe in the Day of Judgement and to believe in Destiny: the inevitable in its good and its bad." And the man said: "You are right." Then he said: "Please teach me about *al*

Ihsan." The Prophet answered: " You worship Allah, as if you are seeing Him, and if you are not seeing Him, surely Allah is seeing you." Then he said: "Inform me about the Day of Judgement—when it will come, the Hour." The Prophet replied: "The person you are asking does not know more than the one asking." Then the man said: "The slave will give birth to his Master; and then you will see people with no shoes, the naked, the helpless, who have nothing, are erecting high buildings."

Then the man disappeared. The person reciting this Hadith stayed there for awhile, stunned. The prophet asked: "Omar, do you know who this person is who is questioning?" Omar answered: Allah and His Prophet know better." The Prophet answered: "He is Gabriel, and he has come to teach you your Religion."

Now, my beloved, know that the Din is a gathering of words of the Way that was revealed in the Presence of the Prophet by the Angel Gabriel, as reported in this Hadith. Islam is Surrender, to be guided in the rules and principles of Knowledge from Allah. The witnessing: "La illaha il Allah wa Muhammed Abduhu wa Rasoolillah." These are the last words from the tongue of the Rasoolillah (Messenger of God), and they encompass the entire Path. (The literal translation of these words is, "There is no god but God and Mohammed is his slave and the Messenger of God.")

We begin to travel with the understanding of al Shariah: the form of the Path. Islam is the Law and the Path, in form and in spirit it is the action of all those who have truly set foot on the Path. It is the action of praying, and the re-ordering of life, which true prayer inspires. This praying is the purification for all the senses, and the healing of all wounds. It is governed by three principles:

1) Atauba: Return to God, Repentance which becomes
2) Taquah: Reverence which becomes
3) Astaqama: Obedience, listening to every word which comes from God, and avoiding everything that is forbidden, returning to the Straight Way.

To purify the appearance is, when deeply understood, to purify the heart. How do you do this?

First by *Atauba*—repentance, asking for forgiveness for what was not right; then through Taquah and Astaqama—not doing again that which was forbidden and living in obedience to every message, to become the embodiment of the Order of God. You purify your consciousness by abstaining from the wrong, and by becoming perfumed with virtue. In this way, you accustom your heart to at-one-ment with Allah. By following the Messenger of Allah in his word, in his action, in his milieu and atmosphere—the fragrance returning to the heart of the rose—you follow the Prophet to the point that all your heart and feeling become blessed and you become enlightened in the Path most dear. In this way, you become knowledgeable—a pillar in the Knowledge of the Shariah al Muhammedee al Mustafaweya, the Way of the Chosen one, the Elevated one; and any person who arrives at the reality which is the Muhammedan Presence never stops doing the Good. The tongue of his presence says, "I hurried to You, my God, and did everything for You, so that You might accept my prayer."

Please beloved, continue the work on the Path. Become persistent, and I urge you not to stop. If you stop, you will be like those who start, and never finish. The Seer and the Path and the person who is walking on it must continue. Please my brother (sister), complete the Way and ascend to the Maqam al Iman al Muhammedee: to the station of the Faith of Mohammed, and Insh'Allah (God-Willing), your Lord will lead you to what He wants and what He accepts. Let us sail by the help of our most dear Prophet, who is in the highest place, and who rows our Boat to the shore of Iman.

The meaning of *Iman* is to believe in the heart, and to assert the laws and principles of Islam from the depth of a living faith, and this is what came on the tongue of the presence of the Dearest (Prophet) in the Hadith just mentioned. Faith, according to us, is the activity of the people on the Path, the hidden (batin) inner Path, of which the center is the heart of the Muhammedan heart. To find it, you must purify all your qualities and human characteristics—your personal presence—to the substance, the reality of the Presence of Mohammed. By purifying your presence from the contamination of wrong, and by elevating it from the mundane world and its bondage to the mundane world (dunniya): using the Light of the Prophet to illuminate a way of passage through the darkness of this world, by living in the essence of the Truth as he lived, and loving Allah as he loved; your presence will reveal itself essentially to be of a spiritual nature. When we speak of the spiritual dimension of the Way of Mohammed, this means that in the purified presence, one is courteous (with Adab) with Allah in all His dimensions.

The Tajaleat, Trust in the deepest sense, is the one apparent characteristic which Allah has given us, and if you follow it, your sense, your consciousness and your heart will rest from anxiety and fatigue. What remains with you is the best of manners, because you sit in the Presence of Allah and His Rasool. Even when you begin to travel on the Path, you are worthy to sit down on the rug of happiness (oonce al hadera), of comfort, of the Presence; and the Iman will flow through you as if it were going through the totality of the universe. First you profess it with your tongue; then it enters your heart; and from the heart it flows to every organ, and manifests through every action; your hand does not refuse, and your ear does not refuse any order which issues forth from the faith within your heart. The faith circulates from the heart to every part of your body until your being is permeated with faith, and then you live in the Garden of Faith. You become calm and full of trust, trusting with yourself, your money, your family; and your faith cannot be shaken by false accusations.

If your faith becomes complete, and your consciousness becomes true, this means that your belief is coming from the Light of Allah, because in this dimension, your faith is the image of the faith of the Messengers. In this faith is a proof beyond reason and science, in accordance with the Knowledge of the Companions of the Prophet who witnessed the belief of the Prophet and the power of Revelation which spoke through him as a consummate proof of the Truth of his Message. What was revealed to the Prophets and Companions was proof from Allah made visible only through the eye of their faith, and this proof infinitely transcends the boundaries of human logic and rationalization. And it is the same with all who follow in the Way of Mohammed; they become immediate witnesses to the Truth from Allah, because he becomes the Eye through which they see, and the Ear through which they hear. As the Prophets are immersed in the Unity of Allah, walking in His Way, because it is their Order, it is our Order to follow their footsteps on the Way.

This is to explain that every person has a station and a rank where he stands at every moment of his journey. For example, one who lives in the station al Wahid encompasses the totality of numbers as well as the parts. He is the source from which the branches and the fruit of the tree come. We cannot speak about the quality of faith which arises out of each station of realization, because it is a thing alive in the chest which the mind cannot articulate or define. One must eat the fruit to taste it. According to the Sunnah, that which judges the faith of a person is the depth of his belief and surrender. These are the two keys which open the door to Knowledge and the things to be known. And these are embedded in the heart of the servant by means of the Fitrah (the innate purity of every being as he was created in the Image of God).

When one returns to his original nature as it was before the contamination of the world, when it was pure, in the pure Vision of the Creator as He made it, he finds in the truth of the natural state the Truth of His Creator and himself. This is the meaning of al Fitrah, that in the undistorted mirror of creation, in the pure Adam, all of the Qualities of Allah are made manifest. Search about your fitrah; then you will walk in the Way of the

Prophets. See the Fitrah in the Din (behaviour) of Ibrahim; it is the essence of Tawhid (Unity). The pure nature of man is the pure nature of God. And know, beloved, if anyone discovers the true essence of the Faith, he does not look to the right or the left. He cannot do anything, except with God, because there is no "he" or "she", and his work is the work of God.

Avoid arrogance and pride, depending upon your own behaviour or your own activity, or any condition of your situation. Do not depend upon your own power or capabilities, but depend upon God, on your Lord, saying:

"O Beloved, Give us Peace: Salaam, and this Peace is You.
You are the Teacher; Please guide me and open the door by Your Blessing and by Your Counsel, and by Your Harmony.
Lead me to the Spring of Your Guidance.
Make my steps strong in the direction of Your Path—the Straight Way to the Presence of the Complete Guide who has inherited the Way of the Truth of Mohammed, my Master.
All the Truth is in Your Hand.
Please do not place me in the realm of choice, but if You give me a choice, I choose what You want from me, my Beloved, my Lord, as You have said, because Your Word is Righteousness, and if You wanted, You would have made all of humankind a single nation, but until this day they are differing, except those whom You have blessed."

Know that no person has ever entered Paradise, the Paradise of Belief in God—Allah, by his own individual acton, but by the Blessing of Allah, from Him and His Generosity.

Beloved, walk with me to the Path of the Highest Good. Hear my voice and follow it to the Presence of God, because life at this time is like the ocean in the time of Noah. When you travel in the Ship of Noah, and you experience this Ship as Faith, you see that the Ocean around you is like the Spring of your Faith; but you need to travel to change your Ship from the Ship of Faith to the Ship of Knowing: al Ihsan, the deep Divine Insight.

The Ocean of Truth is the station of *al Ihsan*: the essence of the Way of Mohammed forever, beyond time. Al Ihsan is the experience of the sincerity of the Truth of Mohammed in everything you do: when you pray—truly to pray, and when you know—truly to know. When any person invokes the spirit of the Truth of Mohammed in his worship, in all his life, he understands what the Scripture means when it says, "Our God is a Living God". The spirits of the Messengers also do not die, but live forever in Him. Everything is from this Spring, and there is no life without this Spring. You can only understand the true *Taquah*: Reverence, when you drink, yourself, from this holy water.

The source and meaning of *Taquah*, the highest good, or the deepest respect, is that you know in Whose Presence you sit. This is like one who sits and serves in the Court of his Beloved, a perfect King, and draws from himself all the veils of his own existence, to give of himself more and more completely to the Presence of his King. Takuah is like the deepest sensitivity; because he fears to be separated from his Beloved for even a moment, and without the Beloved, there is no life. But this reverence, fear and awe are drawn from the well of the deep secret love.

The person who is drawing forth the Hadrat al Muhammedee while he is worshipping, surrendering to do what the Prophet Mohammed taught us, every movement of that person, every stop, every humbleness, every word, every action, and every dimension of his presence is from Allah, by the Power and the Grace of Allah. And if he continues in this Way, all his life is lost and found in witnessing (Mu shehaddah): There is no reality but Him. He gives up his own existence, and his self has no authority over him. The Shaitan (Satan) has ceased to tempt him because this Shaitan has surrendered to him, and he can therefore no longer order him, except toward the Good, and he can not prevent him except not to do the wrong. The purity of his Taquah lifts the veil from the Eye of his heart, to reveal to him where he sits and where he stands, and where he travels; He is in the Paradise of the Presence of his Love.

> "Any person fearing, reverent of the station of his Lord, forbidding himself to go astray, Paradise is his home." *(Holy Qur'an)*

And that person arrives at the station of the servants of God who, when they ask, receive; God gives them what they want because there is no separation between them and Him, and the Giving is from Allah to Allah. This man becomes of those who are unlimitedly blessed—the Prophets, the righteous, the Witnesses, the Good, the Comrades of Allah, and Brothers.

The station of al Ihsan is to be witnessing—seeing Him; to purify one's inside secrets by this witnessing, watching and by knowing the true Knowledge, the Knowledge of righteousness, so that one's spirit ascends from its true station to its truest station. This is the work of the people of the End, though there is no end. In the science of the Presence of Essence, the Essence is pure Vision, and one's body becomes the eye of God. All of the pictures within and without are seen in the Light of reality. You are Adam, when God says to you: "Khaltatoo Adam al Rasuratee" "I created

Adam in My Image." You are the Image of your Lord, but there is no picture, no limit to this Image, because there is no limit to your God, the Supreme.

Understand, because you have achieved (without where and without how, without above and below, without right and left) the Truth, and you are the Truth of Ihsanooka: Righteousness in the direct perception of Him, and therefore you become more devoted to Him, so deeply in love with Him as He is the deep loving within you. You came with the Good, you arrived by the Good, you brought the Good, and what you see you don't see except with His Eye, and He becomes the tongue of your being.

"Wherever you face, My Face."
"You are my Qibla, my Love."
"And wherever you are in the night, take Me as your Protection."

And after that, try to row in the Boat of al Eeqan, the Perfection, the Illuminated Wisdom.

In this station, fear and supplication are one. The fear is inspired by witnessing the Majesty and Wrath and Power of God in the severity of His Judgement (al Jellal), and the supplication is inspired by witnessing the infinite Beauty (al Jemal) of God Himself. In this station, all the polarities are merged in the Oneness, and nothing but the Reality of the One continues to exist. This is a station of the deepest silence; it is the Peace and Silence of the deepest Love, when one has been parted from his Beloved for a long time and finally returns to His Presence; there is nothing to say. As was previously said about those immersed in the Ocean of *al Baadt*, the lover is so much absorbed in drinking the Milk of the Beloved which is flowing from His Lips, there is not a moment to spare in which to speak, or even to remember the Beloved with his voice, but Allah remembers Himself through His slave. The slave thus completely immersed in the Presence of God, is like the light of the essence of a jewel, once the jewel has been broken open, and all its facets returned to the Source and reborn (recreated) in the source of the essence of the Jewel. Through the power of the depth of *al Ishq* (holy consuming love), the soul in the station of al Eeqan returns to the First World and the Pure Being, before the creation of its individuated existence.

Finally, please know beloved, Allah made us. He guided you and me (into being), and there is nothing that accompanies al Tawhid (the Unity)—not any kind of doubt, which by raising it, the united mind can be brought up and down. And there is no objection that can accompany Islam: the surrender to the Will of God, and nothing that can accompany the true Iman to tempt it from the Straight Way, and nothing that can accompany Ma-arifa (deep Knowledge) with accusation.

Please note that al Haqiqat: the Truth, and al Shariah: the Law, are two balances of a scale, and you are its heart. If you leave the heart to go to the side of the Shariah, you become of the Shariah, and you lose the inner Truth of al Islam. If you go to the side of the Truth and abandon the Law, you may break the Law, and this Law is from God. But you are the driver of the Ship, and God asks you about this Ship—how it moves through the sea. For this reason, hold in your hands both the reins. Do not look to the right or the left. Be the Noah of your time.

Know, beloved, while you are in this station, pray for yourself, and be careful with yourself. Do not be careless with the Grace of the Proximity (of Allah). Be aware of the Truth of the Nearness of the Unseen, like a man who sits and serves in the court of a perfect King. In the Presence of the King do not profess yourself to have knowledge, because this knowledge is ignorance, and do not profess yourself to be humble, because this humility is arrogance and vanity. Realize that the witness of Closeness is greater than the knowledge of Closeness. Be silent, and realize where you stand. The true Religion is to witness God the Great by Himself and not by you. Understand.

Sheikh Mohammed Sayad Al Jemal Al Rifai Ash-Shadhulli
Mount of Olives
Jerusalem

NECESSARY QUESTIONS
John Menken

As editor of this volume, I anticipated the privilege of being seen but not heard. But finally, I felt compelled to reflect a little about institutionalized evil. I reckoned no conversation about religion in our time could skirt what Arthur Cohen has called the "tremendum" and has generally been called the Holocaust.

Events like World War II are not private. Those of us who did not directly suffer or participate are called to ponder and try to understand something . . . anything we can about what went on and what is going on.

Still, I am not a survivor and step into this terrain with some timidity. I am touched by Emmanuel Levinas's opening shot in his work *Totality and Infinity.* "Everyone will readily agree that it is of the highest importance to know whether we are not duped by morality." This touches the nerve laid bare by large scale atrocities. But the rawness goes further, to the so-called small evils, those done to children, the weak, the oppressed not in the name of some grand design but simply by "the way things are." This is relevant because it is in the particular "small" evil that the large evil impales *this* vicitm, *this* sufferer.

I was sitting with a dear friend, Ben Marcus, a Taos Indian several years ago in his daughter's Santa Fe house. From time to time we glanced at the final innings of a baseball game on the TV. We didn't say much. The program shifted it seemed without warning to some black and white film footage of the spectacles of World War II. There were images of huge bleak rallies of symbolically dressed mobs, soldiers in rigid lock step,

Hitler snagging the passions of his followers with the rhythms of his mantras, and so on. Ben watched somberly, occasionally shaking his head slightly in disgust and disbelief. He was familiar with these matters. Men from his village had fought in the war. He looked over at me and asked:

"Why was everybody afraid of that fellow?"

For some reason I was dumbfounded at the question. Then he answered it himself:

"They thought he had power. He didn't have power. People thought he did but he could only make people afraid. No one would want to go where he went if they knew . . . his way goes into fear forever. Real power is goodness. When you get up in the morning and watch the sun come up over there . . . the feeling you have then tells about what real power is like. The goodness makes you know good."

The question that we may be duped by, the idea of goodness, has force I think because we live with unexamined auras around the concepts of power, of politics, of morality. Despite the way we may feel there is good medicine in facing the problem of evil in the world.

Today there are varied ways of looking at the Nazi's attempt to execute their aim of destroying the Jews *totally*.

- It is seen as an absolutely unique manifestation of evil whose like has never been seen before. But since it *has* happened once it makes the emergence of a similar evil more easily possible.
- It is seen as related to many other wars in ancient and modern times against the Jews. In this view, the magnitude of the horror is unique but the nature of the evil is not.
- It is seen as related to many other programs of extermination conducted by one group against others throughout recorded history. Sometimes the victims were the Jews, sometimes other distinct peoples.
- It is sometimes seen as a ghastly part of an ultimately benevolent Cosmic Drama.

The way I have listed these options is likely to annoy some readers because it does not do justice to the serious thought invested in each. But space and time are short. One virtue of simplified lists is that they do raise questions.

It is useful here to remember that records of the past show evidence of atrocity as a vicious accompaniment to human history. At the end of the fourteenth century Tamurlane liquidated the entire Nestorian Christian population of Central Asia. In the United States all demographic and population models indicate that during the peak of persecution and armed force against the American Indian probably forty percent of their population was destroyed. Fairly accurate figures show that in 1915 one million out of a total of two and a half million Armenians were destroyed. In the recent Jewish experience, six million out of fifteen million were killed.

When we look at the numbers and percentages of populations murdered it is clear that none of the victims of large scale atrocities are unique. But when we glimpse behind the statistics and try to comprehend we cannot . . .we can only question. In the realm of the particular we are faced in every instance with its own uniqueness.

The common thread of many efforts to find meaning in the Holocaust are either through attempts to decode history or decode Scripture, through using comparative and analogical methods. Do these ventures in comparison help us to act against evil? While preparing his program of extermination of the Jews, Hitler made a well known crack, "Who remembers the Armenians anymore?" This was neither a comparative nor an analogical statement. He simply seems to have been stimulated and emboldened by the fact that people did not remember nor recognize a very recent evil as evil. Intriguing questions are raised by this. David Tracy remarks in his preface to Arthur Cohen's *Thinking The Tremendum* a fact, to him theologically disquieting, that nearly all the murderers of six million Jews were baptized Christians.

A person can never really know the suffering of another in its fullness. Neither can we know with precision the dimension of evil in another time and place. Often it is in the intentionalities of the doers of evil that stakes out the uniqueness of each horror. Comparisons are very tricky when we boil things down to dealing with intentionalities.

When Job's "friends" were trying to invest *his* experience with *their* meanings, trying to weave their own sense of cause, effect, history and analogy into his concrete life, he protested right down to his heels. They could have brought themselves to his situation in a different way but did not or would not.

So, being convinced that morality is as real as goodness, I find another question: What kind of understanding can we bring to anothers suffering or our own that is faithful to our human vocation? To frame this question more relevantly to *The Tent of Meeting Texts*: How can we be faithful to our humanity and our God as members of the community of Muslims or

Christians or Jews?

It seems right here that my American Indian friend's question touches us. For how do we look at our community and how do we look at power? If we place ourselves in community on the wrong foot, we are no longer free persons answerable to the *voice from the whirlwind.* We become individuals reduced by politics or war or some other overriding concern to being mere bearers of "forces that command," forces that are born out of some "larger" purposes that claim to justify a temporary abandonment of ourselves and our consciences. How temporary ultimately is this abandonment? How large are these larger purposes?

Here I willingly fall into the seductiveness of comparison. I see in these "larger purposes" analogies with what may have been meant by St. Paul when he attacked Dominions and Powers, or in the biblical commandment to "have no other gods;" and even in the Koranic injunction to make no "similitudes of Allah."

I do hope though, that the question, if caught on the right foot can lead to rethinking the *givens* of our respective religions. Whether we like it or not the perilous light cast by Mouch or Auschwitz calls us to this.

As I said at the opening of this piece I had anticipated being seen and not heard. I trust that, quite in keeping with that other caste of the "seen and not heard," I have provided some genuine irritation.

John Menken

IS OUR NEIGHBOR VISIBLE?

Dr. Vera John-Steiner

I would like to dedicate this piece to all the people who died either during or as a result of World War II. Their number surely exceeds 20 million human beings—a number that is inconceivable. But it is that war that changed not only my life, but all lives of individuals approaching consciousness by the year 1939.

There were no victors of that war, for the Allies as well as the Axis allowed technology to win over our humanity. Indeed it is that war, and specifically the Holocaust as well as the dropping of the first atomic bomb on civilians, that left us with a heritage that we are just now starting to confront.

In its simplest expression it is the heritage of the invisible enemy. The extreme rationality of the gas chambers made their victims largely invisible, and those who had to get them/us ready for extermination were frequently slave laborers themselves. So our terror was only infrequently witnessed by those who had logically, and with great precision, planned our death.

I was fortunate; as I am a Hungarian Jew who lived in Budapest, I belonged to the last cycle of deportees. And also as a member of a special transport I survived. But perhaps, because I see myself as a marginal victim, one who is aware of my great fortune, I feel even more compelled to live under the shadow of the Holocaust. It is that experience that has made me into a psychologist; it is that experience that I will never fully understand.

On our way to Bergen-Belsen we were marched through a small Austrian town, our jackets clearly marked with the yellow star of David, but the people did not seem to see us. They had seen many such walkers through their town before that summer of 1944, and by this time they had simply ceased to see us. We were seen and not seen by the Austrian men and women in Lintz.

All of us have this "ability" to cease to "see" other people so that they lose their power to affect us as fellow human beings. This "making invisible" of other people is that lesson, or burden, which I see as our most significant heritage of the Holocaust. Because it is only by making one's enemies invisible that we can escalate our abilities as warring nations, more and more with each of the World Wars of the 20th Century. It is precisely for that reason that we are the only species that can consider destroying millions of our fellow beings in overwhelmingly rational, planned and efficiently calculated ways.

These are historical events we are now trying to confront and truly deal with. But the many slave labor and extermination camps such as Auschwitz, Treblinka, Buchenwald, Dachau, and Belsen do have some precedent in previous centuries; genocide is not fully of our times. The extermination of large groups of Native Americans, of Armenians, of child laborers, of religious minorities, of Black slaves, of political opponents in many places and many centuries do indeed give us a precursor of events of this century. But it is our methods that now give us more ability to plan extermination without seeing it. Some of the methods that the German Nazis used, for instance, the walking of victims for hundreds of miles, come from the long walks that Native Americans in 1868 also experienced.

These efforts to put systematic barriers between groups of human beings become more pronounced during war and under other conditions when people become frightened—of death, unemployment, loss of national pride—and these things have affected even this very powerful nation. Thus it is one of the issues that we need to explore more fully when examining the heritage of the Holocaust and its lesson and its lessons for America.

Our technology today makes it possible for us to be much more aware of the existence of millions of other human beings. A sense of the unity of this planet becomes more available to us. But this is not always an advantage, it is also a psychological burden we are not ready to cope with. Our very ability to be aware of each other and of previously "hidden" groups and cultures also creates conflict, tension and anger. We are not ready to think of ourselves as merely one member of very large communities because of our fear of the loss of being a member of a small, unique community. And so we erect extraordinary psychological and ideological barriers to prop up our own threatened sense of identity. This process was exemplified in the Nazi belief that the Aryan race had to be purified. One reaction to their defeat suffered in World War I was an ideology that attempted to create a perception of the uniqueness of the German Aryan race. This was their attempt to overcome the sense of being just one more defeated nation. To achieve this, the Nazi emphasized a sense of *absolute* separation between communities. The ideology of the Master Race created the notion that they had little in common with other people and nations. Further, they tried to differentiate themselves so totally from their *past* history and identity, that only an ideology of complete separation from any other human community met the needs they felt after their military defeat.

I think that this tendency to try to think of one's self and country as unique, following some kind of national failure is a tendency that we cannot afford to ignore in the U.S. today. Whether we admit it or not, we have lost a war. And thus our own need to rebuild our sense of national destiny and uniqueness can reach dangerous proportions. And so I think it is essential to confront ones' recent as well as distant history in a reasonably honest way, if one wants to avoid the process of starting to think of ones' enemies as invisible and to re-write ones' past as a mythology.

Now let me share with you some of the consequences of the German ideology on the men and women who were its invisible victims. The choice of victims who were opposite of the "master race" in many ways—color, facial structure, beliefs, etc.—was logical. But eventually I think that was less important than simply having victims who were invisible.

The consequences of being invisible is that every step of becoming a victim makes you more and more depersonalized. You first lose your home, then you lose your books, then your clothes, then your gold fillings, then your hair; and more and more your personal identity becomes extinguished as you become more and more invisible. The process is well remembered in its early stages by everybody who went through it, but eventually, as Victor Frankl described it in his moving book *Man's Search for Meaning,* the accumulation of these events creates a certain kind of apathy. The experiences become less striking, and peoples' diminished energies are devoted more and more to survival. One danger to this process is that peoples' will to live becomes lost as well.

But there is also a moving literature that demonstrates how people did hold on to their will to live. They maintained it in general by three different sources: (1) religious belief; (2) political belief; and (3) less well known, there were those who were able to hold on to some intense intellectual or imaginative inner life that make it possible occasionally to forget and ignore the immediate realities all around them.

In my own situation I was fortunate because I attended a school where very young people, 10-13 year olds, could have an opportunity to learn this. While countries around us were being occupied, and while people were escaping into Hungary and telling us about the German policies of mass extermination—in that situation the school principal called our parents in to tell them that really all they could do to help prepare us for what lay ahead, was to help us focus more inward and to become more intellectually, emotionally, and imaginatively involved. Our teachers were somehow able to convey to us, and we were all girls, their own sense of passion and belief in the possible existence of human knowledge and civilization while surrounded by all of the darkness.

That brings me to the issue of women as survivors. The ability to test a sense of identity and personhood is often related, especially in men, to professional identity and success or position in the external world. But, at least for the first 50 years of this century, women did not have strongly recognized external status as far as their ability to be recognized as important in the public sphere. But related to this is another tradition that was helpful. That is the tradition of being able to create or re-create families, and provide networks of survival in situations where families were being destroyed. Even young children who were able to attach themselves to a child even younger fared much better than those who had no such possibility.

I believe one of our most important resources for resisting depersonalization is the ability to be nurturant in the midst of brutality. Being nurturant does not only mean that you are strong, it also means that you are honest about your weaknesses. Part of being a caretaker also gives you a relief or release to express your fear and at the same time protect somebody else who's frightened. These two things helped women to survive—reaching out to be nurturant, and being more open about personal fears.

What then have I learned from the Holocaust? What can/must we all learn? I want to conclude with three things. First, the human capacity for nurturance is perhaps the greatest heritage that I brought out of that experience. This is essential and not to be limited to either sex, or to any ethnic or age group or any profession. The human capacity to nurture another human being is perhaps our only passport to planetary survival. All of us have the ability to nurture somebody else. In being able to feel another person's experience we can both enrich our sense of life—bridge the chasm of nothingness—and tolerate, forget, temporarily objectify our own sufferings. We need honest connections between human beings, not based on empty politeness, or on a lack of recognizing real distances and differences between people, or denial of one's history that can be a source of distance. We need connections based on mutual dependence; and since Auschwitz and Hiroshima, this more than ever is essential to our very survival.

Second, we cannot make learning trivial. It is sad that we are making the transmission of knowledge from one generation to another into a very trivial enterprise by constantly making it a measured, competitive, normalized sense of where everybody should be standing, instead of the capacity to transmit knowledge with passion. In order to have an intense inner life under extreme stress conditions, one must have more than the achievements of one's own life; one has to internalize and feel the power of the human heritage, the knowledge of the generations over centuries. So the notion that any one individual has a certain quantity of intelligence, or information, or achievement potential, is absurd when you think of knowledge as a source of life and a will to live.

Finally, I cannot help but repeat that technological development does not necessarily engender moral progress. Indeed, in the 20th century they have become to a great extent opposing forces. Unless we can learn how not to trust our technology, but to take chances to become known to and by our invisible enemies, our technology will win and our human will to survive as a civilization on this planet will be eliminated. I think we are still living in the tradition of invisible enemies; we are still willing to say we have first strike capabilities, rather than trying to maintain the extraordinarily difficult task of detente. If we don't see the people who will be the victims of that first strike as alive, living, fellow human beings, we shall plan our future in terms of military might. Nobody who is a survivor can contemplate that possibility with anything but a desire either to commit suicide or to make an absolute committment to fight that mentality.

Dr. Vera John-Steiner

LADY WISDOM
Marina Warner

And what is her *jouissance*, her *coming*, from? It is clear that the essential testimony of the mystics is that they are experiencing it but know nothing about it.

These mystical ejaculations are neither idle gossip nor mere verbiage, in fact they are the best thing you can read... What was tried at the end of the last century, at the time of Freud, by all kinds of worthy people in the circle of Charcot and the rest, was an attempt to reduce the mystical to questions of fucking. If you look carefully, that is not what it is all about...[1]

Jacques Lacan, Seminar XX

The Wisdom writings of the Old Testament furnish, from within the very heart of patriarchal monotheism's scripture, a body of erotic, feminine and mystical imagery that sets up marvellously reverberating contradictions in a text devoted to the supremacy of a Father God. For feminine nouns predominate in the evocation of divine aspects: *Hokhmah*, the wisdom of God, Sophia, Sapientia, *Ru'ach*, the spirit of God, and *Shekinah*, the shining immanence of God, which overshadows the Ark of the Covenant in Exodus 40:34, sometimes lose in translation, as in Greek *pneuma* or Latin *Spiritus*, the personal, female tenor of the original language.

Hokhmah, Wisdom, is an aspect of the demiurge, and when she speaks, the Godhead appears as a separate female being:

> She is a breath of the power of God...
> nothing impure can find a way into her.
> She is a reflection of the eternal light,
> untarnished mirror of God's active power,
> image of his goodness.
>
> (Book of Wisdom, 7:25-6)

In *Ecclesiasticus*, Wisdom is God's attendant and agent, and the author gives her voice in poetry which beside the Song of Songs ranks with the most voluptuously beautiful in the Bible. She describes her own perfections:

> From eternity, in the beginning, he created me,
> and for eternity I shall remain.
> I ministered before him in the holy tabernacle,
> and thus was I established on Zion...
> I have grown tall as a cedar on Lebanon,
> as a cypress on Mount Hermon;
> I have grown tall as a palm in Engedi,
> as the rose bushes of Jericho;
> as a fine olive in the plain,
> as a plane tree I have grown tall.
> I have exhaled a perfume like cinnamon and acadia,
> I have breathed out a scent like choice myrrh,
> like galbanum, onycha and stacte,
> like the smoke of incense in the tabernacle.
> I have spread my branches like a terebinth,
> and my branches are glorious and graceful.
> I am like a vine putting out graceful shoots,
> my blossoms bear the fruit of glory and wealth...
>
> (Ecclus. 24:3-18)

Writing in Egypt, around 190 BC, Ben Sira, or Siracides, the author of *Ecclesiasticus*, displays the luxuriant imagery of growth and greenness characteristic of Alexandrian allegorizing mysticism[2] to create a figure of Wisdom who is daughter to the godhead ("he created me"), has no mother, waits upon him and does not jeopardize her father's power ("I ministered before him"). He brings her to life in a southern landscape, refracted through the light that makes the flowers blossom and the fruits ripen and causes perfumed sap and oil to flow; we of the north who read the text receive Wisdom's words as hot and exotic, fragrant and spicy in ways to which we are not as accustomed as the Egyptian milieu where the passage was born. But the fertility of the imagery carried the same connotations, and Wisdom ends her praise song by proffering herself to her votaries, as love both maternal and erotic:

> Approach me, you who desire me,
> and take your fill of my fruits,
> for memories of me are sweeter than honey. . .
>
> (Ecclus. 24:19-20)

But the Wisdom writings of the Bible, whilst they softened and stretched the vengeful disciplinarian god of Genesis and Exodus, did not only strike notes of spiritual excitement and rhapsody. The purpose of Ben Sira was practical. In spite of the intense, imagined sensuality of the passage in which she speaks, Wisdom concludes by presenting herself as a moral preceptor, who will lead her followers to live a good life:

> Whoever listens to me will never have to blush,
> whoever acts as I dictate will never sin.
> All this is no other than the book of the covenant
> of the Most High God,
> the Law that Moses enjoined on us. . .
>
> (Ecclus. 24:22-23)

It was passages like this, in which the lovely and inviting Hokhmah presents herself as the ethical guide of God's people, that helped later Christian exegetes to identify divine Wisdom with the Church founded by Jesus. Hokhmah/Sophia, characterized as the bride and spouse of the godhead ("She it was I loved and searched for in my youth;/... I fell in love with her beauty" [Wisdom 8:2], was conflated, in some of the earliest and most inspired allegorical interpretations of scripture, with the beloved and languishing Shulamite of the Song of Songs, ("You are wholly beautiful, my love,/ and without a blemish" [Song of Songs 4:7]. In a key passage of the book of Revelation which closes the New Testament, she was also perceived in the figure of the New Jerusalem who comes down to the wedding feast of the lamb "like a bride dressed for her husband," (Apoc.12:2) and is "clothed with the sun, standing on the moon, and with the twelve stars on her head for a crown." (Apoc. 12:17). This apocalyptic bride, a figure of the saving church, was to become a symbol of great moment, who throughout the mediaeval centuries could inspire meditations on the indwelling female wisdom of the godhead.[3]

Sometimes Jesus, as the Logos, the Word of God, was identified with the expression of divine wisdom, and acquired feminine qualities through reverse-sex metaphors of startling resonance. St. Anselm in the twelfth century and Julian of Norwich in the fourteenth both create memorably personal prayers in which they invoke God as mother.[4] But inspired as their meditations are, they are not representative: in general, the figure of the bridal Wisdom of God, manifest in his Church, was developed by Christian mystics as a separate and distinct female figure, a power with whom, in differing but equally enriching ways, they could establish a personal, intense connection in order to reach closer to God himself.

While Sophia/Hokhmah, the beautiful bride, excited intense responses in both men and women, male contemporaries show a greater need to give her an historical character and to purge the erotic force of the scriptural metaphors by imagining an unimpeachable object of their ardour. The incarnational tendency of Christian imagination led the greatest thinkers of the mediaeval church, like St. Bernard of Clairvaux (d.1153), to identify their bride mother with a mortal, terrestial individual, Mary the Mother of God, and to explore her prefigurement in the Wisdom texts.[5]

Mary's identification with Wisdom is very ancient. In the seventh century, the sensuous verses of Ecclesiasticus 24 had been included in the liturgy to celebrate all women who had consecrated themselves to God and withdrawn from the world. By the tenth century, the Wisdom texts of the Old Testament were also being read on Mary's feasts, and the passage from Ben Sira was included in the first cultic celebration of her, the Saturday Mass. For her nativity on 8 September, also an early Marian feast, the same verses were read, alongside the opening of the Gospel of St. John, thus associating the Word who existed from the beginning with his mother, who, like Wisdom, had also been created 'in the beginning'.[6] For a sermon on that day, St. Peter Damian (d. 1072), one of Mary's early Western enthusiasts, took the Biblical description of Solomon's throne, the Seat of Wisdom (*Sedes Sapientiae*, 1 Kings 10:18-20) and demonstrated its affinity to Mary's virtues: its ivory was white with the whiteness of her virginity, the twelve lions who stood on the Throne's steps were the twelve apostles who gazed up at the mother of God in stupefaction, saying, from the Song of Songs,

> Who is this arising like the dawn,
> fair as the moon,
> resplendent as the sun,
> terrible as an army with banners?
>
> (Song of Songs, 6:10)[7]

Mary still appears under her title *Sedes Sapientiae* over Chartres' Portail Royal, where the child sits on his enthroned mother's knees, as the Logos issuing from Sophia.[8]

Realized figures of speech, exploring the mysteries of redemption through an array of female forms, including the Virgin but embracing a plurality of other figures too, afforded a special pleasure and opportunity to women. The web of allegorical imagery woven by the wisdom texts offered metaphysical writers, like Hildegarde of Bingen in the twelfth century and Hadewijck of Brabant in the thirteenth, a language with an even greater potential for subjective strengthening sublimation than the contemplation of Mary's perfections provided their male counterparts.[9] Early female mystics did not focus on Mary, the maidenly, motherly and humble, with the intensity of their spiritual brothers; and although in their rhetoric they might deprecate women's weakness and littleness, they do not justify their allegorical concept of female Wisdom by appealing to womanly qualities, as Guillaume de Conches did when he commented that Boethius' consolor Philosophia appeared to him *sub specie mulieris*, in the guise of a woman, because "a woman softens the ferocities of the soul, nourishes children with her milk, and is better accustomed to taking care of the sick than men."[10]

It is perhaps surprising that the cult of Mary is less marked in the texts of women writers of the middle ages, that the Biblical passages which sustained her praises in the twelfth and thirteenth centuries were not always applied to her by nuns with the same effusions as they excited in monks. The asymmetry springs from the erotic character of the imagery: votaries' relationship to Sophia, to Holy Wisdom, was changed by the question of sex. In general, while a mystic like Bernard imagined the bride as the object of his love, his contemporary Hildegarde identified herself with the symbol of transcendence itself, not with its worshippers.

In the Latin Vulgate, where "Wisdom" is translated as "Sapientia," it carries connotations of empirical knowledge as well as the mysticism implied by Sophia. Through these intellectual dimensions of the Biblical figure, the Schoolmen of the West had been able to annex pagan culture to Christian purpose. Alcuin, in the ninth century, interpreting the passage from Proverbs, "Wisdom has built herself a house/She has erected her seven pillars. . ." (Proverbs 9:1), identified her house as the house of learning and the pillars as the seven liberal arts, the Trivium and Quadrivium classified by Boethius: the threefold way to Eloquence (Rhetoric, Dialectic and Grammar) and the fourfold way to Philosophy (rather less severe— Music, Arithmetic, Astronomy and Geometry). Albert the Great, applying the same text from Proverbs to the Virgin Mary, wrote that "she possessed the seven liberal arts...perfect mastery of science."[11] Mother Church, assimilated to the figure of Wisdom, could permissibly be represented as the continuator of the classical tradition, the fountainhead of knowledge, practical and mystical, soteriological and historical, as well as the source of the Christian virtues; the Biblical Sophia, and the community of the faithful in Holy Church, could absorb and repeat the lessons of the pagan

Philosophia.[12]

On the Portail Royal of Chartres', on the archivolts framing the Virgin enthroned as the Seat of Wisdom, the Seven Liberal Arts appear to make a clear statement about educational ideals in the twelfth century. Beneath each personified Art, an exponent of genius practises the discipline of which she is the heavenly muse. Most of these great men are classical figures: Priscian for Grammar, Aristotle for Dialectic, Cicero for Rhetoric, Boethius for Arithmetic, Ptolemy for Astronomy, and possibly Euclid for Geometry and Pythagoras for Music.[13] But the female sculptures are strictly emblematic only in one case—Dialectic—who carries a flower and a dog-headed dragon to symbolize good and evil. Otherwise the Arts themselves also practise their skills; Grammar even appears with a raised besom in her hand to discipline the young curly-headed rascals who squat at her knees with their books.

Female education was a possibility, within the clergy at least, and a learned nun, like the Saxon writer Hroswitha of Gandersheim in the tenth century (b. bef. 940, d.c.1002) ,also seized on the opportunity the gendered name of Wisdom—Sapientia—offered. Although she often makes conventional apologies for her sex's failings, she translated her own Saxon name into Latin, calling herself "Ego, clamor validus," "I, the mighty voice [of Gandersheim]," and in the preface to her collection of plays stated clearly: "My object being to glorify, within the limits of my poor talent, the laudable chastity of Christian virgins."[14]

In the play, commonly called *Sapientia*, dramatizing the deaths of Faith, Hope and Charity, her daughters, the women are hypothetically historical characters, real, active, while at the same time they stand as emblematic exemplifications of their sex. When Sapientia is wooed by the pagan Emperor Hadrian, who wants to deflect her from the true religion, he says to her, "The splendour of your ancestry is blazoned in your face, and the wisdom of your name sparkles on your lips." She confounds him and his ministers with her learning, displaying her mastery of Boethius' science of numbers, among other things. When Hadrian tries to force her and her daughters to worship Diana, they refuse, and Sapientia tells Faith, Hope and Charity, "I nourished and cherished you, that I might wed you to a heavenly bridegroom." Faith is then beaten horribly and her nipples are cut off. They spurt milk not blood, like Wisdom herself, who was often portrayed nourishing her followers like nurslings. Gruesome excesses are in store for Hope and then for Charity. After burying her children and praying over them, Sapientia dies as well, but of grief.[15]

Hroswitha, while composing Sapientia's display of erudition, necessarily displayed her own; also, when her sister nuns in the royal abbey of

Gandersheim put on the plays, they enacted a community statement of the strength and fidelity of their sex. In another longer play, *The Passion of the Holy Maidens,* Hroswitha effervescently abandons a high edifying tone and depicts the erring pagan protagonist, Dulcitius, Governor of Thessalonia, falling under an enchantment. Mistaking pots and pans for young girls, he kisses them with passion until he turns sooty black all over. Taken for the devil, he is then beaten up by his own soldiers. But even in this unusual example of a religious farce the undaunted trio of maidens bear allegorical names—Agape (Love), Chionia (Snow-white, the emblematic colour of purity) and Irene (Peace), and when the persecuting Emperor Diocletian says to Agape, "The pure and famous race to which you belong and your own rare beauty make it fitting you should be wedded to the highest in our court"[16] the audience of nuns at Gandersheim—and the performers—would have grasped the intended multiple *entendres*. The metaphor of marriage applies to the relation of Virtues like Love, Chastity and Peace to the Logos. They are the Word's bridal handmaidens, like the new Jerusalem, like the wise virgins who keep their lamps lit waiting for the bridegroom (Matt. 25:1-13). Hrowswitha's farce, influenced by the comedies of Terence to which she had access (she apologizes for their profanity), manages to combine effectively broad Roman humour with the metaphysical uses of feminine gender inspired by the Bible.[17]

The imagery was not confined to convents: courts adopted it as well. The poet Baudri de Bourgueil (d. 1130), hoping to find favour with Adela, Countess of Blois and daughter of William the Conqueror, wrote her a long and learned *ekphrasis* about her bedchamber, which he called her "thalamus," doubtless intending the nuptial overtones. He may have exaggerated its magnificence, and even invented its decor, for his poem records a kaleidoscopic and dreamlike accumulation of furnishings. But even as fantasy, it provides us with a description of how a worldly interior might be appointed at the orders of a woman toward the end of the eleventh century:

> Astiterat dictans operantibus ipsa puellis,
> Signaratque suo quid facerent radio.

> (She herself stood by directing the young women
> at work, and pointed out with her staff what
> they should do.)[18]

Tapestries showing the Creation, the Garden of Eden and the Flood covered one wall; another showed the Siege of Troy and the foundation of Rome. But the piéce de résistance, according to Baudri, was the Countess's bed.

A woven picture of the Battle of Hastings and her father's conquest of England hung at the head, the canopy above was tapestried with the signs of the Zodiac, stars and planets, and around the bed stood three groups of statues representing Philosophia herself with her seven disciples, the Liberal Arts. Carved in ivory, Philosophy's breasts were flowing to nourish her followers, and though she was "full of days," like the primordial church, she was also vigorous, beautiful and unbesmirched, like the bride of the Song of Songs.[19]

A courtly flatterer, hoping for employment at a service in the house of a great lady, thought that such allegorical figures were appropriate guardian angels for her sleep.

Baudri's description sounds fantastic; it probably is. Yet in mediaeval art, Wisdom, the maternal aspect of the Godhead, frequently nurses her adepts like a mother giving suck. She appears, convincingly majestic, in Herrad of Landsberg's twelfth century compendium The Garden of Delights, where the framing *mandorla* around Sapienta distances her from the disciples who drink at the seven streams flowing from her.[20] But the visual arts can dramatize the figure of speech to sometimes hyperbolic effect. When Mephistopheles promises Faust

> "Thus at the breasts of Wisdom clinging
>   thou'lt find each day a greater rapture bringing,"[21]

we do not recoil immediately at the incongruity as we do when we contemplate a manuscript illumination in which Sophia nurses two swarthy, bearded grown men—Saints Peter and Paul—like babies at her breast.[22]

*

A century after Hroswitha, near Wiesbaden on the Rhine, the great seer Hildegarde of Bingen (1098-1178) wrote to a fellow abbess: "The form of woman flashed and radiated in the primordial root. . . How so? . . . both by being an artifact of the finger of God and by her own sumblime beauty. O how wondrous a being you are, you who laid your foundations in the sun and who have overcome the earth!"[23]

This wonderful being, the form of woman in the beginning, preexistent as idea in the mind of the Creator and issuing then from his hand, gave Hildegarde one of the potent, multilayered metaphors that charge her many different writings. Again and again she returned to the sublime beauty of woman as a symbol for human spiritual potential on this earth; she mined both the allegorical tradition of meditating on scripture and late classical philosophical texts, and in her hands allegory became a living, personal form of speech, which still flies across the centuries to ring inspiringly for us today.

The twelfth century, when Hildegarde was writing, marked a pinnacle of Christian humanism, celebrating every soul's potential in relation to a benevolent divine providence. It would never be achieved again so resplendently—not with Renaissance humanism or with romantic idealism. This early humanist vision was fixed on transcendence, while avoiding the damaging dualism that rejects the world as corrupt. In the sculpture programmes, stained glass and soaring arches of Chartres, in the mosaics of St. Mark's, and in long densely patterned texts like Alain de Lille's *Anti-Claudianus,* or *The Rejoinder to Claudian on the Ideal Man*, there exists a dynamic affirmation of this world, with all its weaknesses, flaws and lapses, as nevertheless ordered radiantly and beautifully by its maker.

In Alain's poem, the paragon hero, Iuvenis, or, the Youth, is fashioned by Nature and Wisdom working in partnership, while the Senses and the Virtues, all personified as graceful and maidenly forms, minister and assist his creation, until he is born, the perfect and equally balanced amalgam of matter and spirit.[24] Hildegarde's writings are also representative of her time, in their use of allegory, their close acquaintance with scripture, their frank acceptance of the dignity of the created world, and their ability to take wing up to lofty banks of metaphysical cumulus. But she possesses a unique vision too, and with regard to the uses of the allegorical female form, she is a major writer who continually reaches within these conventional confines to a personal and private place.

The song she wrote to St. Ursula opens with an invocation of the church.[25] "O Ecclesia," sing the three female voices, blended together to praise the beauty of the institute to which they belonged. Hildegarde composed her music for her sister nuns in the convent of Rupertsberg which she had founded and where she lived, wrote and composed, until her death. Their Church has eyes like sapphires, and ears "as the mountain of Bethel" and a nose "as a mountain of myrrh and incense." And her mouth is "quasi sonus aquarum" ("like the sound of many waters"). The sound of the rapidly ascending and descending voices in the recent recording of the song directed by the musicologist Christopher Page resembles the sound of many waters, too. With her music, Hildegarde intended to praise the divine life, both outside her convent and within it, and she did so through the lips of her sisters and the language of oneiric nuptial mysticism taken from the Bible: sapphires stud the throne of the son of man in Ezekiel's vision; Bethel is the name Jacob gave the land Yahweh granted him in his dream (Gen.28:10-19); myrrh and incense perfume the lover's chamber in the Song of Songs. Ursula longs to reject the world and to join the son of God, "pulcherrimum iuvenem," ("a most beautiful youth") in a theogamy, a sacred marriage.

As the voices sing, they reveal to us how profoundly Hildegarde identified herself with Ursula, an English princess of the fourth century who was a beloved saint in Germany. Her story survived in two mediaeval Passions.[26] Betrothed against her will to a pagan, Ursula travelled to Rome on a three-year pilgrimage in order to delay the unlooked-for union. But on her return she disembarked at Cologne, and there, along with eleven thousand virgins of her sisterhood, she was cruelly martyred.[27] Some of their relics were kept in the convent of Disibodenburg, on the Rhine, which Hildegarde had first entered at the age of eight. Hildegarde's contemporary, Elisabeth of Schonau, had received many revelations of Ursula and her companions in 1156-57, and Hildegarde, though she shows no direct influence of Elisabeth's visions, felt sympathy and corresponded with this other German mystic, who like her had renounced the world and lived in a fellowship of women.[28]

Like Ursula, Hildegarde was nobly born, if not a princess; like Ursula, she had decided never to marry; like Ursula, Hildegarde first received visions when she was only five, but kept her experiences to herself. In the song, when the young saint Ursula's longing to marry only her beloved Jesus becomes known, people mock her, as they had scorned the child Hildegarde, inspiring her to keep silent about her own similar desires:

> Innocentia puellaris ignorantis
> nescit quid dicit.
>
> (What simple, girlish ignorance!
> She does not know what she is saying.)[29]

Ursula is then troubled, by an "ignea sarcina" "a burden of fire", like Hildegarde, again, who is perhaps referring here to her own experience, her gift of prophecy. For the young girl's "burden of fire" recalls Hildegarde's account of her own visionary ordeal, described at the beginning of *Scivias (Know the Ways of the Lord),* her autobiography:

> A fiery light, coming with a great blaze out of a clear sky, transfused my whole brain, and my whole heart and my whole breast. It was like a flame but it did not however burn me, but warmed me as it set me alight in the same way as the sun heats anything on which it sheds its rays. . .

And when Hildegarde appears in her own manuscript, in one of the miniatures, tongues of fire are descending on her head, like the flames of Pentecost that gave the apostles the powers of prophecy (Acts I: 3-5)[31]

After Ursula experiences the fire in the song, people recognize her holy vocation and allow her to leave: "Scorn of the world/is like the mount of

Bethel," it continues. So the mount, which in the first verse was likened to the ears of the Church, reappears here as a simile for the cloister; Ursula, Hildegarde and her sisters' counterpart in turning her back on the world, becomes a type of the Church. In the song's beautiful concluding verse, sung in unison, Hildegarde creates, in only a dozen words, a dazzlingly compressed epiphany of the mediaeval doctrine that God's virgins, pearly in their unspotted purity, will triumph over evil:

quia guttur serpentia antiqui
in istis margaritis
materie verbi Dei
suffocatum est.

(for the throat of the ancient serpent
has been choked
with these pearls
which are the stuff of the Word of God.)[33]

She combines with consummate skill scriptural allusions to the wedding feast of the lamb from the Apocalypse, where virgins stand by the side of Jesus, with a daring claim that virginity is consubstantial with the Godhead, and a reminder of God's promise in the Garden of Eden that the serpent will be crushed by a woman, as in the flawed translation of the Vulgate (Gen. 3:15).

*

Hildegarde of Bingen was born in the Rhineland in 1098, the last of ten children. After entering the convent of the Disibodenburg, she came under the protection of the abbess, Jutta of Sponheim, who became the child's beloved foster-mother and teacher. Thirty-one years later, in 1137, Hildegarde succeeded Jutta as abbess, but in 1150 she divided the community, taking with her a small band of sisters, and founded another convent on the Rupertsberg, not far away. She was forty-three when she received the command to write down her revelations. Cloistered all her life, she saw herself as an autodidact, and throughout her wide-ranging works she alludes to herself as "nothing but a poor little woman" (paupercula feminea forma) and resorts to recognizable feminine self-deprecation which rings at the same time with pride and defiance.[34] She also suffered from recurrent painful illness, which caused her bouts of blindness and long spells bedridden and hallucinated; but she distinguishes these afflictions carefully from her visions, for they never caused her pain, or ecstasy, or even loss of consciousness; she did not sleep through them or fall into trance. "Truly I say the visions I saw," she wrote, "watchful I received them, looking around with a pure mind and the eyes and ears of the inner man, in open places according to the will of God."[35]

In the twelfth century, though it saw the founding of the Inquisition to combat the Albigensian heresy in the south of France, mystics who claimed direct communications from God did not suffer the persecutions—and even death sentences—of the visionaries of the late thirteenth and fourteenth centuries. They could cite Biblical authority for their visions: in Joel, Yahweh specifically includes women in his promises:

> I will pour out my spirit on all mankind.
> Your sons and daughters shall prophesy,
> Your old men shall dream dreams,
> and your young men see visions.
> even on the slaves, men and women,
> will I pour out my spirit...
>
> (Joel 3:1-2; AV 2: 28-9)

But the writings of a mystic like Hildegarde were submitted for scrutiny and could be condemned. Her revelations were discussed at the Synod of Trier (1147- 8) by Pope Eugenius III and he issued a qualified approval—perhaps at the urging of St. Bernard of Clairvaux, the greatest metaphysician of a great age, and a political force to reckon with.[36]

Hildegarde was able to continue, uncensored, with the multifarious interests of her own. She was a woman of remarkably wide-ranging curiosity and gifts: she completed three great volumes before she died at the age of eighty-one; as well as composing songs and hymns, she created the first musical drama, the *Ordo Virtutum*, a sung contest between the devil and the Virtues for the possession of a single sinner, the Felix Anima, or happy soul.[37] She wrote scientific treatises on natural history, medicine, and was quite capable of discussing biological reproduction without evasion. In these works, the *Physica* and *Causae et Curae*, she studies the structure of minerals, the properties of plants, the types and character of animals, with a startlingly scientific materialism, radically different in tone from her spiritual revelations.[38]

She wrote commentaries on the Gospels, on the Athanasian Creed, and on the Rule of St. Benedict which she and her sister nuns followed. She corresponded with popes, archbishops, and bishops throughout Germany, with the Holy Roman Emperors Conrad and Frederick Barbarossa, the Byzantine Empress Irene, Eleanor of Aquitaine and King Henry II of England, as well as with many other women who had taken the veil, who wrote to the "Rhenish Sibyl" to put questions of ethics and revelations to her. Many of the letters she received beseech her to pray for the authors; many express longing to see her face to face. The language of Christian fellowship is warm, even extravagant to twentieth century ears. Endearments frame the epistles: she is the best-beloved daughter, a *filia dilectissima*. Hildegarde wrote long, considerate replies, both earnestly pedagogic and radiantly inspired.

Hildegarde saw herself as God's instrument, an Aeolian harp that sang as the breath of God moved through it. She opens her visions either with the phrase "The living fountain says" or "The living light speaks" before she moves into the first person. She compared herself to a sounded trumpet or a filled vessel. She wrote to Elisabeth of Schonau that they were both like "the earthen vessels" filled with the power of God which Paul mentions (II Cor. 4:7) and that the living light of her visions should blow through Elisabeth as it did through Hildegarde, playing on her as if she were an instrument: "So too, I, lying low in pusillanimity of fear, at times resound a little, like a small trumpet note from the living brightness."[39]

But her most memorable and original image for the visionary's relation to God comes from a folktale, not scripture. To another correspondent, a master in theology in Paris, she wrote:

Hear me now hear: there was once a king, sitting on his throne, and around him stood great strong elegant columns, richly decorated, set up with ornaments of ivory, and unfurling all the banners of the king with great honour. Then it pleased the king to raise a little feather from the ground, and he commanded it to fly. And it did as the king wished. The feather flew not because of anything in itself but because the air bore it along. Thus am I . . .[40]

Hildegarde returned to this marvellously eloquent image—the feather on the breath of God—in a remarkable letter she wrote at the end of her life to one of the many people who had been captivated by the personality that shines through her writings. To Guibert of Gembloux, who came to live near her in her last years, she stressed her weakness:

> I stretch out my hands to God, so that like a feather which
> lacks all weight and strength and flies through the wind, I may
> be borne up by him.[41]

But in spite of the utter surrender to His will, Hildegarde also saw their union as cooperation. In a telling passage in her Vita, her last autobiographical work, she describes the task of visionaries to create, shape and define—not only receive—and to show themselves forth as God's work. Taking a metaphor from art, she explains:

> Man with every creature is a handiwork of God. But man is
> also the worker (*operarius*) of divinity, who provides shading
> (*obumbratio*) for the mysteries of divine being... who ought

to reveal the holy trinity to all, since God has made him in his image and likeness.[42]

Hildegarde's writing rarely achieves this shading and transformation through adopting a novel vocabulary or extending her repertoire of images. Instead she mines the same words deeper and deeper until she penetrates through to the anagogical core, and daylight no longer refers to the light of the sun, but to divine goodness, and the vocabulary of female sexual surrender signifies only renunciation in the religious life, and birth the neo-platonist regeneration of the spirit. She rarely applies a metaphor literally; the anthropomorphism of her visions is often ambiguous. But by retaining the language of the erotic life, as so many Christian mystics did, she experiences that life and its energy at the level of imagination, even if the meaning she has attained runs counter to usage in the "real" world. Her mantic powers are never more in evidence than when she praises virginity in the accents of rapture: like a shaman, her words conjure states of being that lie beyond their conscious application. In a particularly fervent letter to another community of nuns, Hildegarde tells the *turba puellarum,* this bevy of girls, to turn their backs on the frivolity, the dancing, the love affairs of the world, and prepare for the eternal dance, the epithalamia and the nuptials of heaven.[43]

For it is as Hildegarde circles in closer and closer to her own story, of claustration in the church's service, that the virginal body of woman becomes her dominant symbol, itself unfolding into a multipetalled cluster of different meanings, emotions, memories, and prophecies. When she exclaimed to the abbess in that letter, "Woman . . .what a wondrous being you are," Hildegarde was trying to justify an aspect of her convent life that had come under criticism. Hildegarde's sisters at the Rupertsberg were famous for the beauty of their clothes; they wore costly raiment, and on their heads crowns—elaborately wrought diadems in niello enamel work in three colours, symbolic of the Trinity, with four roundels showing the lamb of God, an angel, a cherub and a human being. As Hildegarde wrote when she described these circlets, or *rotae*, "This emblem, granted to me, will proclaim blessings to God, because he had clothed the first human creature in radiant brightness. . ." Her justification, granted her in a vision, unites imagery from the Apocalypse of John in the New Testament, Paul's commentary on the splendours of chastity, and the voluptuous drama of the Song of Songs. Her sisters and herself are God's brides; unlike married women, who must only dress in gorgeous clothes if it pleases their husbands, virgins dedicated to Christ have reproduced on earth the primordial state of blessedness they will attain in heaven when they stand, at the last judgement, by the side of the Lamb in garments of white. The state of virginity corresponds to the innocence of Eden, and virgins do not need sackcloth and ashes to expiate worldly transgressions. She could surround herself in her abbey with girls who in their very dress signalled their identity with the holy and the divine.[44]

Hildegarde's writings are filled with conjurations of this ideal girl, queenly, autonomous and beautiful, whom she has brought into being in the enclosed precinct of her convent. The heads of Humility, Patience and Abstinence, in another showing, are also crowned with jewelled circlets;[45] sometimes the Virtues are veiled *more muliebri*, in the fashion of older women, not young girls;[46] sometimes they are bare-headed too, to symbolize their *aperta conscientia*, their clear consciences.[47] She describes her visions of Caritas, the virtue Charity, in another letter, "A most beautiful young girl, her face flashing with such splendid brightness that I could not look at her fully. . . All creatures called this girl *domina*, mistress."[48] Her Charity is winged, but has given her feathers to Humility so she can fly in the *pressura,* the word for the pressure that Hildegarde feels during a vision.[49] As Peter Dronke, the most sensitive and learned translator and exponent of Hildegarde's genius, has written about Hildegarde's Lady Charity: "The allegory unfolded from this vision is about creation and redemption. . . It is when we see these images in relation not only to their allegories but to that image of the bride of God which Hildegarde wanted to embody in her disciples, that certain aspects of her thought cohere in an unexpected way. In paradise, the first woman was created... as the embodiment of the love that Adam had felt. Eve... was initially, in her paradisal state, the glorious *puella* whom Hildegarde describes... and insofar as the virgin brides on the Rupertsberg could still re-enact that paradisal state, they could manifest something of the splendour of this *puella*.[50] They were the living expression of virtues, hypostasized in the real world and freed through inner purity from constraints of reality; their raiment, however elaborate in worldly terms, was a symbolic dress, and she, their abbess, was their *domina* or mistress, like Lady Love herself, winged, in the midst of her visions, with dazzling brightness streaming from her face.

Perhaps such reasoning to excuse pleasure is contrived, or at best deluded; readers may perhaps smile at Hildegarde's living fantasy, her own realization of desires from deeper well-springs maybe than even those from which her visions emanated. But even so, the daring, the quality of high imagination, the fascinating elision between art, faith and life cannot be dismissed; she plundered the common Christian stock of images and showed that, given inspiration, it could be transformed to open the gates of a novel heaven.

Hildegarde was sensitive to the categories of male and female, and her language reflects her distress at the negative value attached to her own sex and its attributed characteristics. Her vision recreated an ideal world in which their strictures were abrogated. She wrote to Bernard of Clairvaux, for instance:

> Ego misera et plus quam misera in nomine femineo...
> I am wretched and more than wretched that I am called woman.)[51]

When she wrote to another fellow abbess on the fall of mankind in the Garden of Eden, she let slip how she endorsed the disparity between the sexes as perceived in her time:

> But the serpent who came breathed eloquent words to the woman, and she received them, and yielded to the serpent. And as she had tasted what the serpent gave her, so she gave the same to her man, and it remained in the man, because a man does all things fully. . . [52]

Latin gave Hildegarde a means of escaping sexual difference and its pejorative charge of femininity. To Bernard she wrote, for instance, apologizing for her lack of book learning and claiming another special power: "Homo sum inductus...sed intus in anima mea sum docta." (I am like a man of no learning...but deep in my soul I am learned.)[53] The resonant opening of her book of visions, describing how she was commanded by God to write, also casts Hildegarde throughout as "homo", "man". Not vir ("male man"), or "femina" of "mulier" ("female woman"), but "homo" the generic, undifferentiated human creature.[54]

Hildegarde needed to sink herself into the generic to escape her femaleness in spite of her combative exploration of symbolic possibilities for the female, because even in the twelfth century, when great ladies enjoyed more autonomy than in the ensuing centuries, and courtly manners accorded women a high place in the scheme of redemption through love, highly influential thinkers were still deeply distrustful of female nature. St Bernard, for instance, in his remarkable rhapsodies on the Song of Songs, recalls the traditional opposition between strength and weakness, and distinguishes damagingly between the symbol of the bride in the Canticle and a real bride, maintaining the rupture that Hildegarde was inspired to mend: "The bride is called beautiful among women," he says, "but women signify carnal and secular souls, which have nothing virile in them, which show nothing strong or constant in their acts, which are completely languid, soft, feminine."[55]

It is not surprising that Hildegarde, whose life's work constitutes a rejoinder to such strictures, characterized Faith herself as a girl, but a manly one, above sexual congress: "Her virginity, which is the Catholic faith, they [infidels] wish to corrupt. But she resists them manfully (*viriliter*) and is not corrupted, because she always was a virgin, and is and will remain so, in the true faith, which is the stuff of her virginity and remains integral against all error. . ."[56]

Hildegarde's extensive writings can sometimes have a scholastic flavour absent from her poetry, her letters and her music, but they also deploy the body as metaphor. *Scivias* teems with personifications to flesh out the mysteries she propounds. But what makes her revelations even more fascinating to us today are the manuscript illustrations she commissioned to accompany her texts. The elaborate figures she described in the book flickered in lavishly applied precious pigments—gold and vermilion, cobalt and magenta—existing in the illusion of art at one degree closer to corporeal reality than the imaginary scenes, figures and actions Hildegarde's writings conjure before her readers' eyes.[57]

Hildegarde herself appears in the first miniature, apparently giving instructions through an opening to her scribe-artist whose head is poking through to listen. She is holding a pen or tablet, while flames descend on her head. The illumination suggest that she sketched out her ideas and handed them over for execution to another, more practised painter. If this is the case, she was able to translate the labile profusion of her visions with quite breath-taking clarity and control of visual imagination. Some of the richly coloured images are intricately enfolded, frame within frame, border within border, pattern upon pattern, as sublimely sensuous and almost as abstract as Hindu mandalas; others exert a different kind of authority over the flux of her words and make intelligible, and even harmonious, some of the more outlandish emblematic details seen by Hildegarde: the scores of eyes on the wings of the cherubim, nearest in rank to the godhead of the nine orders of angels, or the fishing net in which the Church catches souls at baptism.

However "wretched in the name of woman" she was, she vindicated her sex triumphantly with a resplendent sequence of allegories in which the mysteries of creation and redemption, Wisdom, the Church, the Virtues, the souls of men and the sacraments are chiefly represented through female figures. Ecclesia appears most frequently, and she is contrasted with the Synagogue in two full-page miniatures of exceptional power.[58] Hildegarde, who may have been influenced by the anti- Semitic churchmen of her day (like the preacher Benjamin of Tudela), saw the Synagogue:

> . . . black from her navel to her feet, and with bleeding feet, yet surrounded by the whitest and purest cloud, but bereft of

her eyes, she held her hands under her armpits, standing near the altar which is before the eyes of God, yet she did not touch it.[59]

This towering figure, breaking out of the miniature's vermilion frame with her huge feet steeped in blood, keeps her sightless eyes shut and her arms crossed over her breast, as Hildegarde describes, to symbolize her rejection of Christ and her blindness to the truth of his incarnation. The weariness and coldness the painter has managed to communicate in her stance and her face surpasses even Hildegarde's powers of expression in words. The full-scale murex purple Ecclesia, who appears five illuminations later, holds out her golden arms in the *orans* gesture of public prayer and her wide, large-set eyes gaze in melancholy beyond the viewer,"acutissime," ("keenly," says the vision)—out of the side of the acanthus-leaved border. Hildegarde saw the Church as the "image of a woman" of huge size, as big as a great city, with a crown on her head and splendour falling from her arms like sleeves—just as the artist has captured. Ecclesia's fishing net did not cause the illuminator the problem it might have done: he interpreted it as a gold mesh pattern on Ecclesia's body. In the breast of the figure, framed by huge golden plumes like the flames of the inspiration, her several nuns and some priests kneel in a cluster around a praying figure with long blonde plaits. These figures represent virginity and the priesthood, which must exist at the very heart of the Church. It is hardly accidental that the nuns and the central praying girl are dressed and coiffed in the style of Hildegarde and her peers.[60]

Hildegarde of Bingen foreshadows the mysticism of the Flemish Beguines, of Meister Eckhart and Henry Suso in the later middle ages. A campaign for her canonization started soon after her death, but was not successful; her friend Elisabeth of Schonau became a saint, so prejudice against female ecstatics cannot have prevented Hildegarde's own sanctification. There were miracles, however, and a local cult flourished in Germany.[61] Sainted or not, Hildegarde is one of mediaeval Europe's truly original minds. But she was by no means eccentric in the language and imagery in which she phrased her mystical experiences. She stretched a shared vocabulary of her time and deepened its metaphors through her personal commitment to the meaning of her allegorical figures, but they were entirely traditional in Christian thought.

With Hadewijch, the Flemish mediaeval poet of the century after Hildegarde, we find the stream of personal Christian mysticism that flows through the Benedictine and Cistercian movements nourishing the visions of a woman seer to inspire raptures more familiar in their keyed-up, sensuous sweetness than Hildegarde's glitteringly elaborate constructions.[62]

Hadewijch lived in the early thirteenth century in Flanders and may
have come from Antwerp or Brabant. She belonged to a community of
Beguines, religious sisters who did not join convents but remained in the
world and worked for their living. Next to nothing is known about her
otherwise; her works were only rediscovered in 1838.[63] Since then she
has came to be regarded as one of the most important writers of early
Dutch literature because, like Dante in Italy, she chose to write in the ver-
nacular. In her accounts of her raptures, and her letters of spiritual counsel to her sisters, Hadewijch wrought yet another transformation of the
figure of Divine Wisdom, simultaneously the second person of the
Trinity, the Holy Spirit, and Sophia, when she conjured her symbol of
Love—Minne, a female power who courses throughout her writings. For
Minne—Love—is feminine in gender in mediaeval Dutch, like Caritas, or
Agape, but unlike the more familiar Western concepts of Eros and Amor.

In her seventh vision, granted appropriately at Pentecost—the feast of
the Spirit—she wrote of Jesus, "He came in the form and clothing of a
Man, as he was on the day when he gave us his Body for the first time;
looking like a Human Being and a Man, wonderful, and beautiful, and
with glorious face, he came to me as humbly as anyone who wholly belongs to another. Then he gave himself to me in the shape of the Sacrament, in its outward form as the custom is; and then he gave me to drink
from the chalice, in form and taste, as the custom is. After that he came
himself to me, took me entirely in his arms, and pressed me to him; and
all my members felt his in full felicity, in accordance with the desire of my
heart and my humanity. So I was outwardly satisfied and fully trans-
ported. Also then, for a short while, I had the strength to bear this; but
soon, after a short time, I lost that manly beauty outwardly in the sight of
his form. I saw him completely come to nought and so fade and all at
once dissolve that I could no longer recognize or perceive him outside
me, and I could no longer distinguish him within me. Then it was to me
as if we were one without difference . . .

"After that I remained in a passing away in my Beloved, so that I wholly
melted away in him and nothing any longer remained to me of
myself . . ."[64]

The importance of this powerful vision lies in the harmonic shift as
Hadewijch's union passes from sexual transport (repeatedly qualified as
"outward"), to the strong resolution when this outward lover dissolves
into her inward being, and reciprocally, she enters into a state of pure
desire, "orewout"—and melts away into his already annihilated self. In
this "grondeloze grout" this foundation-without-foundation, or abyss-

without-end, the vanishing point of the ego, where it passes through space and time into the boundless infinity of zero, Hadewijch finds her fulfilment.[64a]

Hadewijch does not engage with the historical humanity of Jesus in the manner of her contemporaries—like St. Bonaventure, who lingered lovingly on the circumstances of the Saviour's infancy and upbringing, garnishing the bright image with profuse details in an attempt to make the story of the Redemption work its efficacious magic on the hearts of the audience.[65] She shows no interest in Jesus's biography. He metamorphoses in her visions into a being who belongs in the perspective of eternity on the one hand, an angel or archon, and on the other in her own private processes of self-evolvement. Like Hildegarde, she drew on the allegorical tradition and on the sapiential texts of the Bible to create a range of fictive personal reflections of her ideal self.

In one of the boldest poems she wrote, "The Strongest of All Things," Hadewijch reworked a story that occurs in the First Book of Esdras (included in the Vulgate by St. Jerome, but now to be found only in the Protestant Apocrypha—not the Jerusalem Bible.)[66] A cautionary tale, it issues a sharp warning against the powers of women. The First Book of Esdras relates that once, when Apame, the "favourite concubine" of King Darius of the Persians, "was sitting on the king's right, she took the diadem off his head and put it on her own, and slapped his face with her left hand; and the king only gazed at her open-mouthed." She laughed at him. And he then laughed too.
(1 Esdras 4:29-33)

Hadewijch conflated this anecdote of love and its folly with other stories from the tradition of symposia, in which sages debate the merits of different ways of approaching knowledge, and even added a reminiscence of the legend of St Catherine, who worsted pagan philosophers with her Christian wisdom.

In the poem, four wise masters argue before a king about what could be the most powerful thing in all the world. The first suggests wine, the second says a king, the third says a woman, and the fourth says truth. With some obscurity due to extreme compression, and some forcing of her meanings, Hadewijch develops their reasons: all four answers represent love under different aspects. Wine is sorrow, the sorrow of an unfulfilled capacity to love which leaves the lover suffering from a continual intoxication of "hope and fear."[68] Like one of Dante's torments in the Inferno, the power of this wine binds the sufferer forever. The symbol of the king, the second power, turns topsy-turvy in Hadewijch's verses to become the poor at heart whom Christ blessed in the "Sermon on the Mount," the soul who seeks for no worldly riches or pleasure but "refuses all that is not brought to him by Love."[69] For the third power, woman, Hadewijch audaciously allegorizes the story of Apame's cheeky bid for sovereign authority, sweeping on to say that she is the strongest of all things:

> The reason, which the third master ventured to explain,
> Is that she is truly able to conquer the king and all men.

Hadewijch then gives her a novel identity:
This woman is humility.[69]

She goes on to expound a conventional personification of the virtue as a queen, incarnate in the mother of God, who was so lowly that Love himself, the king of all things, submitted to her:

> She made the Lord a slave...
> ... he fell from his sublimity
> Into this unfathomable chasm.

Hadewijch then turns directly to invoke her audience and tell them that in order to experience the fullness of love they must be prepared to bow their necks to humiliation and obloquy.[7]

But the fourth power—greater than wine, the king, and greater even than Mary—is truth:

> It conquers all
> That was, and is, and shall be.[71]

According to Hadewijch's doctrine, whose taproot runs down to the Bernardine scriptural axiom that "God is love" (I John 4:8), the power of truth is "to live for Love."[72] But what else, besides the Godhead, is "Love" in Hadewijch's thought, but Minne, Lady Love, evoked by Hadewijch's poetic polyphony—Minne, who speaks now in the voice·of the Beloved, of Hadewijch's objects of love as she searches for God, and now in the voice of Hadewijch herself? Her poem concludes with an anthem to this ultimate love, the spirit of truth, strongest of all things, to whom wine, kings and woman must all yield. But they who know this truth are souls who understand all four powers of Love. And, of course, it is Hadewijch, the knowledgeabe exponent of heavenly mysteries, like Dante's Beatrice in Paradise, who has achieved that understanding:

> When the soul loves perfectly
> And truly understands all these powers,
> It loves eternally as it should—
> And as I gladly loved and willed to love.[73]

This is the last time in the poem that she uses the first person pronoun, and it forms a diptych with the first time, both detonating a small shock of surprise at the measure of Hadewijch's claims. At the beginning, she makes it clear that the sages are putting forward knowledge that she shares:

Then each of them expressed my opinion—
Although I was not there then—[74]

And this last time, after telling us

And as I gladly loved and willed to love...

she describes the dimensions of what she means:

Love knows no distinctions;
She is free in every way;
She knows no measure in her functions;
Therefore she cannot heed the purely reasonable truth.[75]

This heedless, unreasonable, immeasurable power of love is greater than truth itself, in its "reasonable" form at least, and again arrives at full plenitude in forgetfulness of the difference between without and within, as in Hadewijch's deepest mystical knowledge of God:

She is no noble and so valiant,
Both in omitting and in doing,
That she considers neither loss nor gain,
If only she returns into herself.[76]

This startling, splendid and profoundly spiritual boast brings the poem to its end. Yet, as a whole, Hadewijch's bravery concedes hints of inadequacy and even humbleness of heart among the asseverations of privilege; she communicates a questing restlessness, not a triumph of complacency.

In the writings of Hildegarde and Hadewijch, the contending strains in Christian thought about women are present but are resolved to produce a remarkably affirmative corpus; they explore the affinities between the idea symbolized and its outward womanly semblance. As the twelfth-century neoplatonist school of realism at Chartres believed, "visible reality reflects invisible reality . . . Thus the symbol contains, in part, the essence of what it symbolizes."[77] In mediaeval allegory, image and idea were conjoined by aptly suggestive resemblance: the lion stands for courage because it possesses the courage of a lion. By analogy, Lady Wisdom or Ecclesia or Minne were no mere mechanical ciphers of wisdom or the Church or Love but in sympathetic connection with their very essence, as both Hroswitha and Hildegarde recognized in spite of their disclaimers of womanhood.

But in the ensuing centuries, the misogynist strain began to cleave image and reality, and the disjunction between women and the positive ideas they traditionally represented in allegory was increasingly stressed. Though it is always perilous to generalize, the decline of this Christian mode of thought and the withering of the mystical poetry that drew its inspiration from the Sapiential books of the Bible were necessary developments before the autonomous abbeys could be brought under control, and such works as the *Malleus Maleficarum* of 1484 could justify the great witch hunt of the Renaissance and codify the alternate, evil, canonical text for the intrinsic wickedness and folly of women.

*

A parallel development in the fourteenth century and onwards also assisted the widening divergence between the use of the female form as symbol and woman as person. The rediscovery of the classical gods, not in itself a misogynist process, nevertheless widened the distance between Lady Wisdom and her exponents on this worldly plane; she began to recede into a mythology thronged by dead divinities, and no longer takes her living place in the ever-present community of the faithful. According to the theology by which a nun like Hildegarde lived, every member of the Church, of Ecclesia, partook of her essence in the here and now, was incorporated into her body, the mystical body of the eternally renewed Christ, and relived his recapitulated redemption, through the ritual of the Mass and the sacrament of the Eucharist. Through each year's liturgical re-enactment every believer experienced the cycle of his life, and so ingested the wisdom of God, itself alive in the world through his foundation, Holy Church. But the Greek and Roman deities, who began to circulate freely as new symbols of the virtues and the arts after the fourteenth century, did not invite identification in the same way; they themselves were no longer actors in a continuously ritual performance of their stories, in which the audience could also join; nor were they commonly represented in the mien of the men and women of the time. Their history belonged in the past, where they were perceived as reflections of an ideal, distant culture. Sophia/Sapientia, leader of the Liberal Arts, as she appears, for instance, in Herrad's *Garden of Delights* or in Nicola Pisano's pulpit in Pisa Cathedral, began to shed her Biblical character and assume the features of Minerva, Roman goddess of Wisdom. Prudence too, one of the four Cardinal Virtues, was increasingly conflated with the same classical goddess, while Fortitude and Justice, the great ladies Lorenzetti had enthroned in Siena's Palazzo Pubblico in the early fourteenth century, like contemporary noblewomen presiding at a courtly joust, were assimilated to Minerva's earlier, Greek counterpart, the chief goddess of classical civilization—Athena. The Liberal Arts become less and less active as they lose their resemblance to allegorized religious virtues practising their skills, and begin to function more and more as classical muses. Grammar no longer disciplines a group of schoolchildren at her knees like a mediaeval schoolteacher, as she does at Chartres; in Joos van Wassenhove's representative Quattrocento interpretation, her sister Music indicates the organ pipes standing untouched beneath her and hands over to the young nobleman, possibly Federigo de Montefeltro, mastery of her subject.[78]

Naamah, credited with the invention of weaving in the Bible, becomes the only female exponent in the fifteenth -century cycles of *artes mechanicae*.[79] Clothworking was a feminine sphere of occupation, and emblematic imagery began to be circumscribed by the limits of female activity rather than expanded to express the transcendent potential Hildegarde so eagerly divined. It was Coluccio Salutati, the leading Florentine humanist, who first classified the Muses of antiquity as counterparts of the mediaeval scholastic curriculum at the turn of the fourteenth century. The Muse was invoked as divine inspiration by Hesiod and Homer in the opening lines of their poems.[80] Named by Hesiod, who says their "one thought is singing," the Nine Muses were only apportioned their spheres of influence much later, in allegorizing Alexandrian scholarship.[81] The Italian humanists rediscovered them, and it is in the guise of classical Muses that the Seven Liberal Arts, under the presiding genius of Wisdom, receive the young Lorenzo Tornabuoni in the exquisite fresco of 1486 by Botticelli for the Villa Lemmi, now in the Louvre. They hold the traditional mediaeval emblems of their calling; but the trivium wear their hair up, like Greek married women, while the quadrivium wear their long rippling hair loose like Korai. The whole company is dressed all'antica, in chitons of diaphanous, swirling light material caught up in folds and overfolds into a cestus above the waist. Lovely as they are, persuasively summoning us to think of higher things, successfully expressing the world beyond, they are ethereal emanations, not solid or even potential exponents of the skills they bequeath upon the youth ushered into their midst.[82] By comparison, Hildegarde's view was fairly fixed in the here and now, before her eyes.

Around the same time as Coluccio Salutati was working on allegorizing Greek myth for Christian humanist purpose, Christine de Pizan (1365-1430?), a devout Christian widely read in classical studies, created a bridge between the new mythology of the early Quattrocento and the mediaeval tradition of female allegory about Wisdom and her children.[83] She tried to retain the language of personification on women's behalf, using it for overt feminist goals. In her *Book of the City of Ladies*, written in 1404, and its sequel *The Book of the Three Virtues*, she continued her campaign to redress the wrongs of misogyny, perpetrated in particu-

94

lar, she considered, by the *Roman de la Rose's* continuator, Jean de Meung, and by Boccaccio in some of his tales of famous women, the *De Claris Mulieribus*.

Christine de Pizan was the daughter of the Italian court astrologer and physician of King Charles V of France. Her father had overruled her mother and insisted that his clever daughter receive the kind of education only a son would normally be granted. She grew up with a wide-ranging knowledge of the classics, of history, and of contemporary Italian and French literature. After her husband died in 1390, leaving her a young and indigent widow, she continued to educate herself, and became the first woman in western letters to support herself, her three children and her mother by her pen, by writing poetry and history, military and educational treatises, and polemical tracts against the detractors of women. She won a committed following among great prelates like Jean Gerson, Chancellor of Paris, and munificent lords like the dukes of Burgundy. She died in retirement in a convent in 1430, probably in the year after Joan of Arc's victory over the English at Orleans, an event that so inspired her she broke the self-imposed silence of her disillusioned old age and composed one of her finest poems in praise of Joan of Arc.[84] In her girlhood and her courage and her faith, Joan had proved the greatness of her sex:

> Hee! quel honneur au feminin
> Sexe! Que dieu l'ayme il appert . . .
>
> (Aah! What an honour for the female sex!
> It's clear the God loves it . . .)[85]

The Book of the City of Ladies had been written nearly a quarter of a century before; Joan of Arc had ridden out of Domremy as the living proof of Christine's earlier argument that God, truth and wisdom were on women's side.

In *The Book of the City of Ladies*, Christine rings changes on the visionary tradition and, purposefully echoing Augustine's *City of God*, she reveals the building of a new sacred city by three ladies: Dames Raison, Droiture and Justice—Reason, Rectitude and Justice.[86]

The stones and fabric of the new city will be the lives and deeds of great heroines and female exemplars as found in ancient history, myth, hagiography, literature and folklore from a wide range of sources. They will give the lie to the traducers of women, so numerous and all-pervasive that at the opening of the book Christine laments—in her "folly"—that she was ever born one.[87] Lady Reason, who directs Christine through her vision, shares the power of consolation with Boethius's pagan Philosophia and the insight and beatitude of Dante's Beatrice in Paradise, a poem Christine was the first to mention in French; but she also turns up-side down Jean de Meung's Dame Nature from the *Roman de la Rose*, a text Christine had bitterly rebutted in some of her earliest writing. Dame Nature represented for Meung the biological necessity of the race to reproduce, the carnality and consequent inferiority of females as the members of the species instinct with drives to procreate. Christine in her book coolly but cogently deploys her contradiction of Dame Nature. For what could be more rational, spiritual, well-behaved or wise than Ladies Rectitude, Justice and Reason?

Christine's paean to her sex culminates in praise of Mary, the Queen of Heaven, who is brought to the City of Ladies by Justice to be its sovereign, for she is "the head of the feminine sex" and the reason that honour must be paid to women. Thus Christine reverses the more usual strictures that Mary was the exception among women, the pure among the impure, the only one fit to be mother of God, and makes her the essential type of fe-male virtue and the proof of women's worth. Then Justice addresses Mary:

> My Lady, what man is so brazen to dare think or say that the feminine sex is vile in beholding your dignity? . . . Since God chose His spouse from among women, most excellent Lady, because of your honour, not only should men refrain from reproaching women, but should also hold them in great rever-ence.[88]

Christine can be repetitive and frequently didactic in the scholastic manner; but she was a startling pioneer. She is the first writer of her sex to coalesce the image repertoire of classical antiquity with Christian sym-bolism. In her work, as in the first harbingers of the pagan retrieval (like Alcuin), Mary and Minerva fuse as the highest representation of woman. Like much later Renaissance classicists who interpreted mythology as prefiguring Christ, Christine in France perceived no split in the con-tinuum between the goddesses and the Christian redemption. In *The City of Ladies*, Minerva, like her Greek avatar Athena, presides over the culti-vation of the olive, the art of weaving, the forging of armour and the play-ing of flutes; but in Christine's tale, she is the historical inventor of these arts and others, including shorthand. Lady Reason explains her to Christine:

> This maiden was of such excellence of mind that the foolish people of that time...said she was a goddess descended from Heaven . . .through her ingenuity she invented a shorthand Greek script in which a long written narrative could be tran-scribed with far fewer letters...a fine invention whose discov-

ery demanded great subtlety.[89]

She goes on to describe how Athena first gave armour to the Greeks, thus betraying a historical conflation of Minerva, the Roman deity, and her Athenian predecessor. She describes how the mistaken cult developed.

> After her death they erected a temple in Athens dedicated to her, and there they placed a statue of her, portraying a maiden . . .

But by denying the goddess's divinity, Christine could with impunity introduce her into the feminist continuum of heroines and great creative intelligences.

Christine de Pizan was a Christian who annexed Athena-Minerva as one of her predecessors in wisdom and skill; in the invocation with which she closes *The Book of Feats of Arms and Chivalry*, a treatise on right conduct in war composed some six years after *The City of Ladies*, Christine entreats Minerva to help her with her undertaking:

> O Minerva, goddess of arms and chivalry, who by virtue of understanding far surpassing other women discovered and established the use of forging iron and steel among other noble arts . . . Adored lady and high goddess, do not be displeased that I, a simple little woman, who is as nothing compared to the greatness of your famed learning, should undertake now to speak of such a magnificent enterprise as that of arms . . .

She continues her prayer—to this woman whom only "foolish" people had mistaken for a goddess—by playing on Minerva's fellow feelings:

> Please look on me kindly, for I can share in some little way the land where you were born, which was formerly called Magna Graecia, that country beyond the alps now called Apulia and Calabria, where you were born, and so like you I am an Italian woman.[90]

For Christine de Pizan, the centuries since Italy was a part of Magna Graecia had elapsed but in the winking of an eye: Minerva was her reflection, inspiration and compatriot. In a manuscript of the time, Christine and Minerva are positioned side by side, like friends and allies.[91]

Dame Reason is an allegorical figure, a figment of Christine's special pleading on behalf of women. But Minerva, the source of wisdom, had lived as a woman in Christine's view. Christine does not relegate her to the symbolic order, but acknowledges her reality, as Homer acknowledged

Athena's. Christine cannot unpick the tangle of belief and knowledge in her work, which winds together the Wisdom figure of the Bible, the fountainhead of learning represented by the goddess Athena-Minerva, and the incarnate and historical individual Mary into a paragon who is also a type of the female sex.

From the vantage point of a learned and sophisticated court in the early Renaissance, Christine could marshall the conventions of female allegory and their foundation in the accidents of grammatical gender, and support her argument for women in a polemical and open discourse that Hildegarde of Bingen in the twelfth century did not attempt. Hildegarde never articulates the argument as overtly; she was a visionary, and her unconscious carries her towards a vatic imagery of self-revelation and self-affirmation that Christine, who was pedagogic by taste, chose deliberately and consciously to adapt.

Christine's is a more modern voice, the single authorial first person, and the autobiographical, even confessional passages in her writings anticipate the innovations of the next century. By contrast, Hroswitha and Hildegarde, and Hadewijch too, in their very different situations and at diffrent times, nevertheless share the communality of their first person voice; they belong to a group and they speak with the voices of their fellow nuns, and not just to them. Hildegarde imparts information as she retells the messages of her "living light," but she presents herself as a conduit, a sounded vessel, connecting earthlings to heaven. She and her hearers accept her as a link, not an isolated and embattled advocate. Nor do Christine's exemplary ladies move and act in such extended involving rituals, liturgical and theatrical, which both Hroswitha with her plays and Hildegarde with her music were able to create; Christine's persuasiveness suffers from her isolated position, the comparative difficulty for a mediaeval pioneer feminist like herself to realize her allegories in the courtly society in which she lived, in spite of her success as its chronicler and ungarlanded poet laureate.

Two hundred years before, Hildegarde of Bingen had harvested a store of imagery for a community of friends and sympathizers who shared it with her and were in the main in agreement with its latent praise of all human creatures' relation to the divine. But Christine de Pizan's voice is defensive and insistent, and foreshadows the modern artist's predicament, alienated from the consensus of the world, who attempts from within to generate a world view that will share that consensus, but finds she cannot, plead as she might. Perhaps that is why Christine de Pizan in her later years in a convent fell into the silence that became so much more customary for women than the brilliant, confident loquacity of Hildegarde of Bingen.

Female allegories which press upon us more noisily today than Hildegarde's or Christine's are informed by a different spirit and a different appreciation of the potential of women.

*

When Prince Albert was overseeing the designs for the new House of Parliament, he made a small but significant change in the classical sculptor John Gibson's monument to Queen Victoria, which still stands in the Prince's Chamber of the House of Lords. Gibson had proposed that the enthroned queen should be flanked by seven-foot-high allegorical statues of Justice and Wisdom. It is a reflection of the pressure that notions of femininity had brought to bear on the convention of female allegory that Prince Albert thought Wisdom not entirely appropriate, and suggested that she be replaced by Clemency, "as the sovereign is a lady." "I was pleased with this idea," commented Gibson.[92]

In the middle ages, the Wisdom figure and her manifold meanings had proved a vehicle of transcendence for women; in the early Renaissance, Christine de Pizan had invoked as an ally the goddess of learning and art, Minerva. But however great a virtue mercy is, Albert's substitution on behalf of his wife the Queen betrays all unthinkingly how drastically the great mediaeval image store of female definition and possibility had been depleted in the century which precedes our own and has done so much to shape us.[93]

Marina Warner
London, England

1. Jacques Lacan, *Seminar XX, Encore.* "God and the Jouissance of The Woman" (sic) A Love Letter." (1972-1973), in Juliet Mitchell and Jacqueline Rose, *Feminine Sexuality, Jacques Lacan and the Ecole Freudienne.* (London, 1982) p.147.

2. See *The Jerusalem Bible*, intro. to the Wisdom Books. pp.1034-35.

3. Jean Danielou, "The Church", in *A History of Early Christian Doctrine before the Council of Trent.* Trans. and ed. John A. Baker. (London, 1964) pp.293-313 on early theology about the Church as the Bride of Christ; see also Roland Batey, *New Testament Nuptial Imagery.* (Leiden, 1971); Herbert Musurillo, *Symbolism and the Christian Imagination.* (Baltimore, Dublin,1962) pp.18-19; for Shekinah, see *Encyclopaiedia Judaica.* (Jerusalem, 1971); 14, cols 1349-54. Marina Warner, *Alone of all her Sex: The Myth and Cult of the Virgin Mary.* (London, 1976). pp.123-31; Phyllis Bond, *"Images of Women in the Old Testament"* in Rosemary Radford Ruether, ed. *Religion and Sexism.* (New York, 1974) pp. 41-88.

4. The dedication of Sancta Sophia in Constantinople was to the Second Person of the Trinity, not the Holy Ghost, as a Western European might assume. See Anselm, "Prayer to St. Paul" in *The Prayers and Meditations of Saint Anselm.* Trans. and ed. Sister

Benedicta Ward, S.L.G. (PC, 1973) esp. pp.153-6:

"And you Jesus, are you not also a mother . . .
Fathers by your authority, mothers by your kindness.
Fathers by your teaching, mothers by your mercy."

See Julian of Norwich, *Revelations of Divine Love*. Trans. and intro. Clifton Wolters.
(Penguin, 1966) passim, esp.p.170:

He needs to feed us . . . it is an obligation of his dear motherly love. The human
mother will suckle her child with her own milk, but our beloved Mother, Jesus, feeds us
with himself. The human mother may put her child tenderly to her breast, but our
tender Mother Jesus simply leads us into his blessed breast through his open side, and
there gives us a glimpse of the Godhead and heavenly joy... This fine and lovely word
Mother is so sweet and so much its own that it cannot properly be used of any but him,
and of her who is his own true Mother -and ours."

The metaphor of God's motherhood is warranted by several passages of the Bible. See
Isa. 66:13; 31:5; Ps. 27:9-10; Luke 13:34-35; Matt. 23:27. Meditations and studies on
this subject include Caroline Walker Bynum, *Jesus as Mother: Studies in the Spirituality of the High Middle Ages*. (California, 1983) and Margaret Hebblethwaite, *The
Motherhood of God*. (London, 1984). I have also benefited from correspondence on this
subject with Dom Sylvester Houedard, to whom much thanks. In April 1984, the sculptor Edwina Sandys interpreted the scriptural passages in visual terms, to create a
"Christa", a crucified Jesus with breasts for the Church of St. John the Divine in New
York—a good example of the flexibility of language compared to the dismaying literal-
ness of image. *Times*, (April 26, 1984)

The third person of the Trinity was also sometimes attributed feminine gender; see
Elaine Pagels, *The Gnostic Gospels*. (New York,1981) pp.61-62; and Warner op. cit.
pp.38-39; also Martin W. Meyer, *Making Mary Male: the Categories "Male" and "Female"* in the Gospel of Thomas, *"New Testament Studies"* (forthcoming).

5. See Etienne Catta, "Sedes Sapientiae," in *Maria,* ed. Hubert du Manoir de Juaye, S.J.
Vol.VI. (Paris, 1949-71), passim; Musurillo op. cit. pp.81-3; Warner op. cit. pp.128-9,
pp.197-8.

6. In the *Shepherd of Hermas,* a second century visionary text, the Shepherd sees the
Church "full of days" like the figure of wisdom.

7. Peter Damian, "Sermo in Nativitate Beatae Mariae Virginis," in *Patrologia Latina* ed.
J.P.Migne (Perugia) vol.144, cols.735-40; see Gertrud Schiller, *Iconography of Christian Art*. Trans. J.Seligman. (London 1971-2). Vol.I pp.23-4.

8. Adolf Katzenellenbogen, *The Sculptural Programmes of Chartres Cathedral*. (Baltimore, 1959) p.15 pl.9. Mary was also represented as a type of Wisdom herself, not only
as her Throne. See the beautiful Jesse tree in the Lambeth Bible, c.1150, in *English
Romanesque Art 1066-1200*. Cat. Hayward Gallery, 5 April - 8 July 1984. Ed.George
Zarnecki, Janet Holt and Tristram Holland. (London, 1984), pp.114-5.

9. Two early examples of the high incidence of female personification in works either
made or commissioned by women: the Cross of Lady Gunhild, daughter of the king of
Denmark, commissioned by her in c. 1075 (in the Danish National Museum, Copenha-
gen), shows Ecclesia and Synagoga, Life and Death in the roundels on the arms. Life and
the Church are robed as Gunhild herself might have been - *Ivory Carvings in Early
Medieval England 700-1200*. Cat. Victoria and Albert, May 8 - July 7, 1974, pp.44-45;
the tapestry of the abbey of Quedlinburg, worked by the nuns in the twelfth century,
tells the story of the marriage of Mercury and Philology, based on the popular allegory
by Martianus Capella of the fifth century. The surviving fragments represent such
scenes as the embrace of Mercy and Justice.

10. Guillaume de Conches, Ms. Paris BN Lat. 14380. Trans. and quoted in Joan M. Ferrante, *Woman as Image in Medieval Literature*. (New York and London, 1975) . p.43.

11. Alcuin, De Grammatica, J.P. Migne, Patrologia (henceforth PL) Vol.101, Cols. 849-53. Quoted Henry Adams, *Mont-Saint-Michel and Chartres*. (Princeton, 1981). p.93.

12. See Incipit in Alcuin's revised Vulgate, BM. Add. Ms. 10546 f.262b; and another, opening Ecclesiasticus, in the Bible of St. Martial de Limoges BN Lat. 8 II fol. 74 v. in Marie-Therese D'Alverny, *La Sagesse et ses Sept Filles*. Pl.II between pp.262-3.

13. Katzenellenbogen op. cit. p.16, figs.9, 24.

14. Hroswitha, *The Plays*. Trans. Christopher St. John. (New York, 1923) pp. xxvi-vii; see Peter Dronke, *Women Writers of the Middle Ages*. (Cambridge, 1984), pp. 53-83, for his characteristically perceptive account of her writings.

15. Hroswitha op. cit. p.137.

16. Ibid p.35.

17. See Dronke op. cit. pp.72-3; 77-9.

18. Baudri de Bourgueil, *Les Oeuvres Poetiques*. Ed. Phyllis Abrahams. (Paris, 1926). Poem CXCVI, lines 103-4. The poem is 1365 lines long, pp.196-231.

19. Ibid. 949-1342.

20. See G.J, Witkowski, *L'Art Profane a l'Eglise*. (Paris, 1908-1912). Vol.I, 195, (Bourges Cathedral) and Erich Neumann, *The Great Mother*. Pl.175, for examples of Wisdom nursing.

21. Goethe, *Faust*. trans. Philip Wayne. (1949), London 1984. Part 1, Faust's Study (ii), pp.93-4.

22. Vat. Lib. Ms. Pat. Lat. 1066. See Neumann op. cit. Pl.174.

23. Hildegarde, in PL Vol.197, Col.338. Trans. Dronke (1984) op. cit. pp. 165-6, slightly adapted by me. For Hildegarde in general, see Peter Dronke, ''Hildegarde of Bingen as Poetess and Dramatist'', in *Poetic Individuality in the Middle Ages* (1970) pp.150- 92; Dronke (1984) op. cit. pp.144-201, 231-64; Dom Louis Baillet, ''Les Miniatures du ''Scivias'' de Sainte Hildegarde conserves a la bibliotheque de Wiesbaden'', in *Monuments et Memoires. Academie des Inscriptions et Belles Lettres*. Ed. George Perrot and Robert de Lasteyrie. Vol.XIX. (Paris, 1911) (Fondation Eugene Piot) passim.

24. Musurillo, op. cit. pp.150-1.

25. ''Sequences and Hymns by Hildegarde of Bingen'', recording by Gothic Voices, directed by Christopher Page. (A 66039). My thanks to Patricia Morison for communicating her love of this music to me. See Dronke (1970) op. cit. pp.161-3.

26. Dronke. Ibid. pp.163-5

27. This famous example of what seemed to the reformers the fallaciousness of Catholic cult was the result of a copyist's error. He understood XIMV to mean 11,000 Virgins (XIM V) rather than eleven Virgin Martyrs.

28. PL Vol.197 Cols. 216-8; Dronke (1984) op. cit. p.149. See Lina Eckenstein, *Women under Monasticism*. (Cambridge, 1896) pp.256 ff, 274 ff.

29. Page recording op. cit.; Dronke (1970) p.162.

30. PL Vol. 197 Col. 383.

31. Baillet, op. cit. p.56.

32. Page recording op.cit.; Dronke (1970) p.162.

33. Dronke, ibid. gives "For in these pearls/ Of the substance of God's word/ The throat of the serpent of old/ lies strangled." Latin text, pp.202 ff.

34. Dronke (1984) op. cit. pp.201.

35. Hildegarde of Bingen, *Scivias*. Ed. Adelgundis Fuhrkotter and Angela Carlevaris. (Corpus Christianorum XLIII-XLIIIA). (Turnhout, 1978), 1.1.

36. St. Bernard of Clairvaux to Hildegarde, PL 197. Cols.189-90.

37. Recording by Harmonia Mundi (HM 20385/96) directed by Klaus L. Neumann, (St. Michel de Provence, 1982). See Dronke (1970) op. cit. pp.169 ff pp.180-92.

38. Dronke (1984) op. cit. pp.171-183, pp241-50 for edited passages, cf. her discussion of physical "virtues" or powers in PL 197, Cols. 847-8.

39. PL 197, Cols. 216-8; Dronke (1984) op. cit. p.149.

40. Ibid. Col. 352; see also Page's record sleeve notes, which first brought this letter to my attention.

41. Dronke (1984) op. cit. p.168; he gives the Latin text of the letter pp. 250-254.

42. Hildegarde Vita. Ibid. pp.236-7.

43. PL 197 Cols.371-3. Letter to community of nuns at Zwiefalten, nr Wurtemburg. Cf. her vision, quoted Dronke (1984) op. cit. pp.164, 239, of a "Pulcherrimus et amantissimus vir".

44. Dronke (1984) p.169.

45. Hildegarde, *Scivias* 1,4, PL op. cit.

46. Ibid. III,3, PL op. cit. Vol.197, Col.592.

47. Ibid.

48 Hildegarde, *Letter to Abbot Adam of Ebra*. PL 197 Cols.192-3; Dronke (1984) op. cit. p.170.

49. Dronke, ibid. p.145; he gives the Latin text of Hildegarde's Vita pp.231-64

50. Dronke (1984) ibid. p.170.

51. Hildegarde, *Letter to Bernard*. PL 197 Cols.189-90.

52. Hildegarde Ibid. Cols.325-6

53. Hildegarde, *Letter to Bernard*. Ibid. Cols.189-90.

54. Hildegarde, *Scivias*; see also the passage from Vita, Dronke (1984) op. cit. p.231.

55. Bernard, *Sermo XXXVIII,iii, 4, In Cantica Canticarum*. Quoted Ferrante, op. cit. p.28.

56. Hildegarde, *Scivias* 2, III, PL 197 col. 453.

57. The illuminated ms. of *Scivias*, one of the great treasures of the twelfth century, was lost in Dresden, where it had been taken for safe-keeping, of during the last war. Baillet, op. cit., passim, reproduces many of the illuminations, some in colour.

58. Baillet, ibid. PLs. V, VII.

59. Hildegarde, *Scivias*, I,V. 14-33, PL 197 Col.433.

60. Baillet, Pl. VII; see also *Scivias,* Fuhrkotter and Carlevaris ed., pp.174 ff.

61. David Hugh Farmer, *The Oxford Dictionary of Saints.* (Oxford, 1978) p. 193.

62. For Hadewijch see *The Complete Works.* Trans. Mother Columba Hart OSB. (London, 1981) pp. 1-42; Ria Wanderauwera "The Brabant Mystic Hadewijch", in Katharina M. Wilson, *Medieval Women Writers.* (Manchester, 1984) pp.186-303. also Hadewijch d'Anvers. *Ecrits Mystiques des Beguines.* Trans. Fr. J.B.P. (sic) into French. (Paris, 1954) pp.7-56; Dronke (1984) op. cit. p.325 for bibliography; Suzanne Lilar, *Aspects of Love in Western Society.* (London, 1965) pp.90- 100; and Tanis Margaret Guest, *Some Aspects of Hadewijch's Poetic form in the "Strofische Gesichten".* (The Hague, 1975) (Though this is principally a technical study).

63. Hadewijch, trans. Hart, pp.1-2.

64. Ibid. Vision 7, pp.281-2.

65. Lilar, op. cit. p.99.

66. See Bonaventure, *Meditations on the Life of Christ.* Trans. Isa Ragusa, ed. Isa Ragusa and Rosalie B. Green. (Princeton, 1961).

67. Hadewijch, "The Strongest of All Things". In Hart (ed.) op. cit. 1. 25, p.319.

68. Ibid. 1. 466, p.320.

69. Ibid. 11. 48-51.

70. Ibid. 11. 62-74.

71. Ibid. 11. 75-76.

72. Ibid. 1. 77.

73. Ibid. 11.85-8, Hart p.321.

74. Ibid. 11. 4-5, p.319.

75. Ibid. 11. 93-5, p.321.

76. Ibid. 11. 97-100, p.321.

77. Ferrante, op. cit. p.38.

78. In the National Gallery of Art, London, part of a pair showing Music and Rhetoric, reproduced in *The Rival of Nature* (Cat.). NGL (London, 1975) p.47 Nos.251,252. The rest of the cycle have disappeared. For Naaimah or Noemi, and her brother Tubal-Cain (Gen. 4: 2) the originator of metallurgy and musical instruments, see Michael Evans, "Allegorical Women and Practical Men: the Iconography of the Artes reconsidered" in Derek Baker, ed. *Medieval Women,* (Oxford,1978), p.327.

79. Homer, *Odyssey.* Prologue, 1-10; *Iliad,* 1; Hesiod, *Theogony.* 1-25; *Works and Days.* 1 ff.

80. Hesiod, *Theogony.* 56 ff. Hesiod's Muses are Clio, Euterpe, Melpomene, Thalia, Erato, Terpsichore, Polyhymnia, Urania, and Calliope, and the spheres they were later allotted are respectively, History, Elegy, Tragedy, Comedy, Lyric, Dance, Music, Astronomy and Epic. See James Hall, *Hall's Dictionary of Subjects and Symbols in Art.* (1974) (London, 1984), though definitions do vary. See Ibid. p.217, for their attributes. Hesiod gives them two different accounts of their origins: daughters of Kronos, they later reappear, engendered on Mnemosyne (Memory) by Zeus.

81. See Guilio Carlo Argan, *Botticelli.* Trans. James Emmons. (1957) pp.101-7; the frescoes form a pair with another, showing Lorenzo Tornabuoni's bride Giovanna degli Al-

bizzi being led to meet the Virtues or the Graces.

82. There is a sarcophagus in the Glypothek Munich showing Minerva and Apollo standing together in the centre, at either end, with the Muses between them. Another in Woburn Abbey, shows Apollo and Minerva together in the centre, with seven muses.

83. Ovid, *Metamorphoses*. Trans. Mary M. Innes. PC. (1955) 5, 250 ff p.123.

84. Cicero's *Letter to Atticus*, saying that a statue of Athena is especially appropriate for his study, was interpreted to warrant her patronage of the intellectual life.

85. For Christine de Pizan, see Earl Jeffrey Richards' introduction to *Book of the City of Ladies*. Trans. Richards, (New York, 1982) pp.xix-xxvi; Sarah Lawson's introduction to *The Treasure of the City of Ladies or The Book of the Three Virtues*. Trans. Lawson. (London,1985) pp.15-27.

86. *Christine, Le Ditie de Jehanne d'Arc.* Eds. A.J.Kennedy and K. Varty.(Oxford,1977).

87. Ibid. p.44; see Marina Warner, *Joan of Arc. The Image of Female Heroism.* (London, 1981) pp.220, 63, 25.

88. There are also reminiscences of The Shepherd of Hermas, (see *Hermas Le Pasteur.* Trans. and ed. Robert Joly, Paris, 1968), in which the Church appears to Hermas, the visionary of the title, as a woman, and then unfolds a series of visions in which various personifications, maidens all, build the Church on earth.

89. *Christine* (1982) op. cit. pp.3-5.

90. Ibid. p.218.

91. Ibid. pp. 73-5.

92. Ibid.

93. Christine, *The Book of Fayttes of Armes and Chivalry.* pp. 7-8.

94. Ibid; see Warner (1981) op. cit. Pl.11.

95. T. Matthews, *The Life of John Gibson.* (London, 1911) p.175. Quoted *Works of Art in the House of Lords.* Ed. Maurice Bond. (London, 1980) p.38.

96. Contemporary Christian feminism has returned to the feminine scriptural imagery, to work new meanings. In 1984, Rosemary Radford Ruether issued a call:

As Woman-Church we cry out . . .

We are not in exile but the Church is in exodus with us. God's Shekinah, Holy Wisdom, the Mother-face of God has fled from the high thrones of patriarchy and has gone into exodus with us. She is with us as we flee from the smoking altars where women's bodies are sacrificed, as we cover our ears to blot out the inhuman voice that comes forth from the idol of patriarchy. As woman-church we are not left to starve for the words of Wisdom; we are not left without the bread of life. Ministry goes with us too into exodus . . ."

R.R. Ruether, "Reflection on Woman-Church." *Probe.* Vol.XII, No.2. Feb/March 1984. p.3.

PRINCIPALITIES AND POWERS
Lynne Bundesen

Each woman's story bears witness
to God in her life and God in her times.

The particulars often vary.

I am a woman, not unlike others of my time.

Since the age of three I have been fascinated by, hypnotized by, controlled and served by religion. Through experience and images I have learned something about the nature of God and about the temperment of principalities and powers.

The experiences may all be mine. The images, are collective.

It was on the day—a very particular day—I encountered the doctrine of original sin that I first lost my innocence. I was three. I was in nursery school; the scene was milk and cookie break.

Women who had chosen to serve their church by administering its theology were the instruments for conveying the doctrine of original sin.

I can still see myself standing at the edge of the long brown folding table where the milk cartons with straws in them stood in orderly rows and I can still feel the tremor through my body as I was accused of having ordered white milk and taken chocolate or of having ordered chocolate and taken white. I was Eve and the milk was the fruit of the knowledge of the tree of good and evil.

There I was, locked in the coat closet for the rest of the

morning, my privileges and my freedoms gone.

All light had disappeared.

There I was, crammed in with wet leggings and muddy boots, punished for God knows not what.

The punishment, it seemed, was to be perpetual when I rode my tricycle home, crossing the alley next to our flat and was hit by a speeding car driven by a "heathen", the Chinese operator of the local hand laundry around the corner.

I knew how to add two and two.

I knew then there was a direct relation between the milk and the accident.

A collection of images and sensations overwhelmed me as I lay there twisted up in the tricycle, looking up at the twisted branches of the tree.

I remember the view from the ground up through the branches and I remember the color of the blue-grey sky. I remember thinking I was watching some kind of slow motion movie of a girl lying on the grass and the girl's neighbors and nanny running to pick her up. I remember thinking how interesting this all was and how complicated life had become.

Now, since I had been educated into the results of orignal sin, my human history was entangled with the principalities and powers present in the middle decades of the twentieth century as surely as my body was entangled in the crushed tricycle.

There was the church and the school and I was to learn later, the government. There was good and evil and right and wrong and sin and punishment. There was this life and life hereafter and maybe someplace that wasn't either.

Before then I was innocent. The first three years of my life were pre-Eve. Nothing separated me from the sky. After the accident I suffered and got up again the next day and behaved as if nothing unusual had happened.

Along with original sin, crucifixion and resurrection became part of my day to day life.

I had many more encounters with scholastic theology during my school years. I wanted to know God.

Some years later I was, both literally and figuratively, living in the desert and the waste howling places.

I was experiencing a wilderness far removed from scholastic theology.

Much of life was involved with the crops and with the laundry and with reading the Bible.

One day, while in the desert, after the wash was finished I carried it to the line to hang the sheets up to dry. As I pinned one corner of the sheet to the line and gathered up the linen to pin the other corner the sheet was dry. In an instant, in a twinkling of an eye, the wet sheet dried. I pinned another and gathered the remainder of the fabric. Looking through the fabric I could see women throughout time washing linen on rocks by a river. I saw it with my eyes. There was no time. The women were there in front of me and the sheets were dry before they were put on the line.

Nothing I thought before that moment seemed true to me. How is it possible to see women through sheets? Everything I knew seemed open to re-evaluation.

Where once I looked at my watch there was now no time. Where once I was alone in the desert I was now one with women throughout all time and all cultures. I had changed my thinking. I had repented.

Where once women had instructed my thinking into sin, punishment and the loss of freedom, women now had shown me through the sheets that I was not a prisoner.

It was that very night that I was lifted by force from my wilderness.

Literally and figuratively I drove out of the desert, out of the dry places, to the ocean. One more crucifixion and one more resurrection.

The milk of babes, twisted tree branches, sheets whiter than any fuller on earth can white them; collective religious symbols, images and events mixed together in my life as they have for other people in other times and other places.

I am tied to all those who have seen twisted branches as a symbol of the cross. With those who know that milk means innocence, those who know that linen sheets are not to wrap the dead but to provide resting places for the living.

I stand somewhere in a tapestry illustrating life.

As I live my life I add fibre and thread to the tapestry. I add some color here, some texture there, here some shading, there some foundation.

The particulars of my experience do not separate me from my fellow humans. They bring me into union with them.

My life is woven through with the lives of the prophets and the lives of the deaf and mute and blind. It is linked to the life of the woman of Samaria; bound to the lives of saints and sinners, to the lives of all people through all time.

I have come through tribulation with much hesitancy and complaining into glimpses of the promised land.

I am one of the children of Israel.

I know my life more completely as I come to know other stories, other lives.

Together the stories repeat the one story of the male and female of God's creating—the male and female—apart from principalities and powers.

Lynne Bundesen

VIENNESE COYOTE
Richard Erdoes

When my mother was pregnant with me my father told her: "We won't let him be a Jew. Jews are discriminated against. Anti-semitism is on the rise."

My mother said: "I won't have him raised as a Catholic. Confession is a nuisance. Then there is the matter of birth control and, god forbid, he should ever need a divorce."

They decided that I should be baptized as a Protestant—the only Protestant in a family which was half Jewish and half Catholic. But then Tante Poldi married a Protestant; and Berlin was a Protestant city. Out of thirty-two kids in my class, two were Jewish, two Catholic and all the rest Protestant. Religious instruction in school was still obligatory. On Luther's birthday the whole class was taken to Wittenberg to hear a preachment in the Schlosskirche, the very church onto whose portal in 1517 Luther had nailed his 95 Theses. Later we were taken to the Wartburg where a bearded Luther had been hiding out under an alias. We were shown the room where he had thrown an inkwell at the devil who was trying to tempt him, shown the spot on the wall made by the ink (and on the sly, a sulphurous yellow spot where the frantic fiend, trying to flee from the enraged reformator, had broken wind). Later we all had sung: "Ein feste Burg ist unser Gott." Protestantism might feed the soul, but it did not feed the belly. Protestant Berlin was starving. I grew skinnier and skinnier. It was decided that I should be sent to various branches of the family, where food was still plentiful, for some fattening up.

My first "fatter-uppers" were Uncle Sandor, the stationmaster, and his wife, Aunt Maya, the ex-milliner from Cracow. They lived, at the time, in Pernhofen-Wulzeshofen in lower Austria—"hicksville," a place, as the saying went, where the foxes and the rabbits said good night to each other. The only reason it had a railroad station, of which my Uncle was stationmaster, was the nearby sugar factory which needed trains to transport its product. Pernhofen was a typical "Strassendorf," a village consisting of a dusty, unpaved road lined on both sides with the peasants' houses, each an exact whitewashed replica of its neighbor. Slightly larger than the others was the Wirtshaus, the inn, in which, among much uproar, incredible amounts of alcohol were imbibed. Aunt Maya had her six acre "farm" right near the railroad station.

Uncle Sandor was a socialist and atheist. Aunt Maya, on the other hand, was exceedingly pious. Every morning at five o'clock she went to early Mass. Every morning she came back full of fleas. As I had the sweetest blood in the family, all the fleas were on me within the hour. I had to learn the proper technique to catch them, such as taking off my shirt in a jiffy, stretching and flattening it against a lamp so that the flea could be seen as well as prevented from jumping about, and then deftly reaching in and grabbing it. Before taking the flea out from the flattened shirt in order to "knack" it between two fingernails, it had to be "wuzelt," that is, rolled vigorously between thumb and forefinger to tangle up the legs so that the little devil could not jump away. Another technique was to go to the brook, disrobe completely, turn all garments inside out, shake them out over the water, and then run like heck. The best technique was one perfected by the local doctor. When he saw me scratching he would spray a whiff of chloroform into my pants and sleeves, tell me to shake them forcefully and make off before the little buggers came to.

Aunt Maya was horrified to learn that I was a Protestant heretic. "You poor boy," she wailed, "condemned to hellfire everlasting! You poor lamb! As a Catholic you could be bad, steal a little, get girls into trouble. It wouldn't matter. You confess, get absolved, you are free from sin again just like a newborn babe. What good is it that you are a good boy, not trying to feel under a girl's skirt, telling the truth, getting good marks in school. You won't get the credit for it. Your good works will be wasted!"

Aunt Maya kept strict accounts of her good works. Whenever she gave a dime or some grub to a poor hobo, she would immediately look up toward heaven and mumble: "Have you seen it, Lord, put it to my account!" She discussed my case with St. Jude, her favorite saint. I heard her talking to him about me through the thin walls separating our rooms. She taught me to say my "Ave Maria's" and dragged me to Mass, dipping my fingers into holy water, guiding my hands in making a cross. As extra good works she set up a table before our house with plaster statues of Christ, Holy Mary, and St. Jude. On the feast of All Souls a priest came to say Mass at Aunt Maya's altar—right before her door—and ten soldiers in parade dress had to kneel before it and then discharge their rifles into the air. Afterward, the soldiers got Wurschteln and a seidel beer; the priest and the corporal, fried chicken and a glass of Karlowitzer.

Aunt Maya's only reading matter was the weekly "Kirchenblatt," the church paper. "Come here, Richard," she said one day. "I'm going to read you something. Here by the petroleum lamp." The story she read me was about a mishap in a chemical factory. The factory had huge metal vats and, from time to time, the stone-hard chemical residue had to be scraped off the vats' inner walls. Workmen were put to this task with hammer and chisel. At a given signal the workmen left the vats. One man did not hear the whistle. To his horror, a lid came down and screwed itself onto the vat. Water and chemical fluid poured into the vat through a hole, rising to the poor man's nostrils. Then the fire was kindled beneath the vat. Suddenly the foreman saw white steam escaping from the side of one vat. He hurried to see what was amiss. To his horror he saw a little finger emerge from a small opening in the vat, beckoning frantically. The fire was extinguished, the lid unscrewed and the poor victim lifted out—saved at the last moment, more dead than alive.

"What is the moral here?" asked the church paper. It was this: even if help had come too late the workman's suffering would have lasted only a very short time, while the unconverted heretic and Jew would boil and burn in all eternity. Also, the workman still had a tiny bit of control over his fate: he had his hammer and chisel, could make a hole in the vat, could wiggle his little finger. There would be no chisel or finger wiggling for the condemned souls frying in their hellish vats in chemicals way over their nostrils.

I was impressed and frightened. After all, this was printed. I was only eight or nine years old. I still believed in the printed word. I was ready to be converted. Anything, but those eternal bubbling vats. But just then it was "back to school," and Berlin. "Next time," said Aunt Maya, "don't worry."

But there was to be no next time. Next time, came Budapest and grandfather Josef—to put some fat on my ribs. I did not like Budapest where I spent the whole of my eleventh year. Aunt Irma, my father's sister, was a cold woman who had no way with children. I was forever in the way. I had to be absolutely quiet because of the endless singing lessons. Uncle Graeff was still teaching, Aunt Irma accompanying him on the piano.

Scales, scales, scales, up and down , until my ears were ready to shrivel up. I was not allowed to bring up friends unless on special occasions, such as my birthday. I was fed up being sent to relatives and places I did not like, being forever shifted from one place to another, giving up friends and familiar surroundings. I transferred some of this dislike to the city and the whole country.

It is said that the Balkan begins wherever the Turk has ruled over 150 years. By this criterion Hungary is a Balkan country. I have always loved the Balkans, Yugoslavia for instance, with its oriental flavor, its wonderful half Turkish and half Slavic music, its dances, its national costumes, its Roman and Byzantine remains, its coastal cities, magnificent little Venices, its Moslem provinces with their mosques and muessins calling to prayer from the top of slender minarets. For the sake of these things, I gladly accepted other characteristics of the pre-World War II Balkans—vermin, dysentery, filth.

Berlin was Prussia and Prussian discipline made me uncomfortable. It worshipped the army and the uniform. It was chauvinistic and, even at an early age, I did not like any of this. But Prussia was also clean and vermin-free. Civil servants were almost incorruptible. People wer punctual; everything functioned.

The Hungary of the twenties, to me, seemed to combine all the bad of Prussia and the Balkans, without any of the good. As one of my friends put it later: "Hungary—that's Prussia with bedbugs." This view was unjust, as I found out later, but came pretty close to how I regarded it at the time.

My grandfather was kindly, but aloof. He took me to the synagogue which impressed me by the absence of plastercast saints. He taught me the "Shema Yisroel" and a few half-Yiddish, half-Hungarian songs:

> Sholet bonlach unterm bed
> Kis angyalom
> Man hat auch schon den Schidach geredt,
> Kis angyalom
> As der Schidach nicht ward san,
> A Krenk dem schadchen in pippig heran,
> Kis angyalom!

which translated means:

> Sholet beans under your bed,
> My little angel,
> The marriage has been all settled.

If the marriage won't take place
A sickness into the marriage broker's navel.
My little angel.

Hungarian Jews had a superstition that sholet beans put under a young girl's bed would help getting her a bridegroom.

Nagypapa—"Grandpa"—would take me to Kugler-Gerbeaux, a fantastic sweet shop in the city park for the "dobos torte," or Marillen knodlachs. He took me to the top of the old fortres hill on the Buda side, he bought me a pair of ice skates, but most of his free time he spent playing cards with his cronies. He spent more time with the Jeshive Bocher—the young Talmudic student he fed and housed for charity's sake—than he did with me. He said: "It's all right for you to eat a little ham, provided you don't do it in the apartment, and you don't have to fast on the 'long day,' because you are a good Goy." I did not like that, because I did not like to be excluded; it made me feel lonely.

When summer came a man appeared in imposing livery. He was the groom of a Grof—the Count De B._____ a powerful magnate with a manor house and large estate in Pasaret not too far from the capital. The groom brought an invitation from the Count to spend six weeks on his country estate. The Count had been an admirer of my father. Aunt Irma and Uncle Graeff were flattered. In due time, a carriage arrived to convey me to the Count.

Prewar Hungary was, in a way, still a medieval country. Officially it was still a kingdom. The joke went:

"What is Hungary?"
"A kingdom."
"Ah. Then it is ruled by a king."
"No. It is ruled by the regent, Admiral Horthy."
"By an Admiral? Then it lies on a coast and has a navy."
"No. It is nowhere near an ocean and, therefore, has, of course, no navy. The Rumanians have occupied and stolen half of Hungary."
"Then Hungary and Rumania are enemies?"
"No. They are allies against Russia."
"Hungary has a strong army then?"
"By the treaty of Trianon, Hungary is forbidden an army and may have no universal service."
"Ah. No army and no draft."
"On the contrary. The army is everything. Everyone must serve!"

And so on, and so forth.

The Court's estate was a feudal demesne. The Herr Graf was always dressed in full gala with a sash across his chest, a diamond cross of the Knights of Malta sparkling on his breast. He was very impressive-looking in an inbred, elegantly imbecilic way, and, to me, effusively friendly. I immediately was assigned a servant for myself and a pony, called "Buckshi" like Aunt Maya's calf. The Count had a fantastically beautiful nutbrown daughter of fifteen, "Magdi" by name, who mothered me and allowed me to fondle her.

The Count was a most generous man. He had a smorgasboard—an enormous table laden with a variety of innumerable goodies—going twenty-four hours a day, and about a dozen guestrooms ready for instant occupancy.

These were held in readiness for actors and actresses, opera and movie stars, poets and painters who were allowed to drop in at any time of day or night to stay, eat and be merry for as long as they pleased. The actresses arrived with their lovers, the tenors brought their mistresses. There were stables with horses for them to ride, dully gleaming guns in racks for them to go on a shoot, tennis courts and, even, a swimming pool—a sort of gigantic above-ground bathtub.

The chief servants, the estate manager, the head gardener, the butler, and Miss Magdi's tutoress were all Germans ; native Hungarians, in the Count's opinion, being incapable of filling such responsible positions. The manager, the gardener and the butler had been given handsome cottages for themselves and their families. The slave work was done by Magyar peasants who owned not one square inch of soil, because all the land as far as the eye could see belonged to the Count. Then, accompanied by the estate manager, the great magnate appeared on one of his infrequent inspection tours, all the peasants and their womenfolk hurried to kiss the hem of his jacket. Once I went into the attic of the manor house, entering into the room which contained many dummies draped with the Count's costumes which he wore on state occasions. Among the brocaded outfits were velvet and stiff silken dolmans, gold braided "atticas"— Hussar's jackets never to be worn but to be draped over one shoulder— fur and silk caps with egret plumes, boots of red and yellow Morocco leather. On the walls hung heavy, curved Turkish sabers, their hilts of silver encrusted with garnets and turquoise. The whole place looked like a theatrical costume shop except that the silver and turquoise, the marten, sable, and leopard furs were for real.

Young as I was, I could see clearly that the Count's generosity as a patron of the arts was paid for with the sweat of the peasants whose wives and daughters casually submitted to the embraces of the Count, his male relatives and guests, because it was an ancient custom for them to serve the sexual needs of their betters. Often at dusk, I saw the peasant women go together to the river to bathe. They never took their clothes off. With their high boots, skirts and blouses on they would wade into the water up to their chins, chat a while and then come out, dripping, empty their boots and march home, singing.

The village had an outdoor movie. Half a dozen bedsheets sewn together and stretched between two tall trees served as a screen. Whenever the wind blew into it, all movements were distorted as the billowing sheets rhythmically expanded and contracted the shapes of the actors. I remember seeing one Jackie Coogan, and one Pola Negri, film.

At the end of my stay the Count took me around the shoulder and said, "My dear boy, I loved your father. He was a wonderful man. I tell you this: if you ever find yourself in trouble, come to me. I can fix any kind of trouble you might get into—for your dear dead father's sake." Fifteen years later I had occasion to hold him to his promise. I remember our last talk together in 1938. He did not like my politics, but he disliked the paperhanger who had taken over Austria even more.

"My dear boy," he said, "I belong to the anglophile Count Teleki party and the Germans will kill me one of these days. (They eventually did put him into a concentration camp.) My kind of world is dying anyhow. It might surprise a young whippersnapper like you to hear that I, too, am an admirer of Voltaire, Diderot, John Locke, even Thomas Paine. But you see, dear boy, the trouble with revolutions is that the stinking untutored peasants, the drunken factory hands, and god forbid! the half-civilized petty bourgeois canaille, always want to take a hand in it. Beware of one thing above all—the aristocrats in rags and the guttersnipe in tailcoat and top-hat. Revolutions should be made only by the noblemen for the benefit of nobles, by the Orloffs, Mirabeaus, Lafayettes, Washingtons (as a descendant of Saint Elizabeth of Hungary), the Lord Byrons. Never let dumb common folk get mixed up in it. They spoil everything!"

"Dear Count," I reminded him, "I, too, am common folk."

"No, never." he protested, "as far as I am concerned, all good artists and poets are noblemen."

My next fattening-up station was Sarajevo. One of my mother's cousins happened to be a retired engineer. He had built virtually all the iron railway bridges in the provinces of Bosnia and Hercegovina, of which Sarajevo was the capital. Up to 1870, the whole area had been Turkish, from 1870 to 1918 it belonged to Austria, and after that it became part of Yugoslavia. Most of the inhabitants of the two provinces were, and still are, Moslems. The bridge builder had fallen in love with a girl from a Muslim family, carrying her off as his wife. Thus we had relatives by marriage in Sarajevo. Compared to Berlin, Bosnia was a land of milk and honey. I was invited to spend a few months with a "Musliman" grand uncle.

Uncle Alijah was a bearded patriarch, a "Hadji," who had undertaken the obligatory pilgrimage to Mecca; also an expounder of Koranic law at the Husruf Pasha Medresse. With him lived his wife, Aunt Hajkuna, and Nada, his alluring granddaughter. In everyday life, they spoke Serbo-Croatian, at home, Turkish, in the mosque, Arabic, and to me, the quaint and scurrillous Austro-Hungarian bureaucratic German. So, I had no language problem. Uncle Alijah was given to much sitting in the sun, nodding, thinking, gazing, expounding and relaxing. He always smiled benevolently, even in his sleep. His skin was like old parchment, but his eyes were still sharp and clear. On Fridays, Uncle Alijah took me to the Begova Dzamija Mosque. Before the mosque stood a fountain and a large wooden rack with square slots, each slot contained a pair of slippers. He pointed one of them out to me: "These are for you. Every slot has a number. Remember yours." He made me wash my feet and put on the slippers, then we went in. Inside, the mosque was bare—in a way resembling Grandpa Joseph's synagogue. No pictures or statues anywhere, just soft carpets covering the whole floor, a frieze of illuminated letters—quotaions from the Koran along the tope of the walls—old brass and glass lamps hanging from the ceiling and the finely carved mihrab—a sort of pulpit—on one side. Uncle Alijah taught me to recite: "Allahu akbar, la illala illala, Mohammedi rasul ulla." He gave me a handful of dinars to hand to the poor outside, quoting from the Koran: "Wherefore oppress not the orphan; neither repulse the beggar; but declare the goodness of Allah."

During Ramadan, we waited for the boom of the cannon on Alimegdan Hill, announcing the end of day and of fasting. Uncle Alijah did not always trust the guys with the gun. If in doubt, he would hold up two thin threads to the window, one white and one black. As soon as it was dark enough so that he no longer could distinguish the black from the white, that was the exact beginning of night and feasting. Uncle Alijah instructed me to watch for tourist unbelievers smoking during the daylight on the streets during Ramadan, telling me sternly to be sure to knock the pipes, cigars and cigarettes from their mouths. I said I would do it, but did not dare to carry out my promise.

Aunt Haykuna taught me to sing:

"Crven fesitch, mamo . . .

A red fez give me, oh mother..."

And:

"The Drave River is burning,
Its waters are aflame
Woe, aflame and burning
Is our wezir
Two walis
Four beys
Eight aghas
Sixteen onbashis
Twenty-four mudirs
And a whole regiment
Of Bashi-Bazouks,
Burning, set aflame all
By beautiful Esnina's eyes."

Nada's eyes were like that. "Black as leeches," as Uncle Alijah said, paying her a high compliment. Or, as the uncircumcised Croat peasants put it:

"Eyes has the girl, aj, black as my feet!"

Nada usually went around dressed in native Bosnian garb—in "pumphosen," white, baggy, belly dancers' trousers; "opanken," slightly upturned brocade slippers; a silken blouse and a tiny, gold-embroidered vest.

Once, Uncle Alijah invited guests who played the tamburitza and the button accordian. Aunt Hajkuna got carried away and suddenly broke into a high, trilling, ulalating cry which made the hair on my back stand up. It was a sound I heard Sioux women make many, many years later during an American Indian movement action. They called it the "Brave Heart Song." Aunt Hajkuna had a Turkish name for it, something like zilgit.

"What does it mean, Auntie, this cry?" I asked her.

Her eyes were no longer dull, but flashing: "We make this sound to encourage our men in a fight and when we clean up the battlefield."

"Clean up the battlefield, Auntie? Clean up, how?"

"You see," she said in her funny royal-imperial Austrian German, " in the old days, long ago when I was still very young and good to look at, we lived way down south in Sulimanovo, our village was all Musliman. The next village was St. Sava, just a few miles away, all Christian. In both villages they spoke the same language, wore the same kind of clothes, worked the same tiny stony fields, herded the same miserable spavined sheep and goats, suffered the same poverty. But once every lifetime, or so, there was a massacre. Nobody could figure out what brought them on, suddenly, without a reason.

"Well, one night, after a feast day, I think, when we were all asleep, the St. Sava men came over in the wee hours and started cutting throats. They had rifles and pistols, too. They took us by surprise. We bided our time for a whole year. Then in the night after their feast of St. Sava, when we knew they'd be blind, stinking drunk after the Christian manner, it was the turn of our men to cut some throats. And us women and girls went along. And during the fight we opened and lifted our blouses to show the heros the delights awaiting them if they did well. And we made this trilling sound which made the men fight better, and we took our sharp knives and cleaned up after the men."

"What do you mean Auntie, clean up?"

"Oh, how stupid you are! Cut off the unwashed, uncircumcised male things to stuff them down their throats, what else?"

"Their wee-wee's ! You don't mean it, Auntie! You couldn't do such a thing !"

"I sure could, and I did," said Aunt Hajkuna, caught up in a nostalgic reverie. "You got to do it, you just have to. It takes their strength away. And that of their sons, and the sons of their sons, for generations. They'd do it to us, too, if they had a chance. Aj, aman, those were still men in the old days."

'Yes," Uncle Alijah piped up. "you Austrians don't know how to fight. During the war you always ran away. The only ones to run faster were the Italians. Did you ever see a Bosniak run away?"

And yet, Uncle Alijah and Auntie Hajkuna were among the most gentle, peaceful and hospitable people I ever met.

Uncle Alijah often took me to the Bashczarzcija —the old bazaar and market place—and to the street of the copper and brass workers where men haggled for hours over the price of a single item, sipping thick black coffee with rose petals swimming in it from tiny cups. The haggling, Uncle Alijah explained, was great fun, a wonderful way to pass the time. He also took me on outings to the Neretva River where water from the rapids was used cunningly to turn a number of spits, each with a lamb carcass rotating slowly over a bed of coals. One simply cut off a hunk of meat and broke off a piece of bread from oversized loaves, and that made a fine meal. The weight of the chunk of meat determined the price—just a few pennies. Uncle Alijah also walked with me through the old Turkish cemeteries made up of white headstones. And suddenly, one day, it was time to return to Berlin. "Peace be with you," said Uncle Alijah, and placing his hands upon my head, "remember, God is great and there is no God but God."

This ended my fattening-up journeys to far-flung relatives in foreign lands, because shortly after Sarajevo, the food situation in Berlin and Vienna returned to normal. I had been fattened up with Protestant konigsberger klopse, with Catholic speckknodel, Jewish beef flanken with horseradish, with aristocratic Hungarian porkolt, and Islamic raznici—skewered bits of grilled lamb. In the process, I had become something of a connoisseur of international cuisine.

Religion worried me, though. I had learned to pray in four different ways; had been taught to eat pork and not to eat it; to worship the images of saints and to abhor them as graven images; learned to keep Sunday sacred, but also Friday and Shabbes; had been told to drink wine and to shun it; to knock cigarettes out of the mouths of unbelievers smoking during Ramadan. When was I supposed to fast—during Ramadan—at the Day of Atonement—should I abstain from meat on Friday and eat fish instead when I so disliked fish? Devotees of all four faiths with whom I had come into contact had made it clear to me that salvation could be attained only through one way: their own specific way, to the exclusion of all others. Whom was I to believe? Which God was the right one?

In Berlin, the planetarium had just been opened. Uncle Willie took me there. Upon the vault of the roof I saw projected the firmament with its constellations and numberless stars. A lecturer explained that our own Milky Way galaxy alone contained billions of suns, each presumably with its own attendant planets.

What an incredible relief! God had been represented to me as a kind of Prussian drill sergeant, forever mad at being incorrectly worshipped. I now concluded that whoever, or whatever, ran this universe of billions and trillions of suns and earths could not possibly be so narrow-minded to care, or even have time to notice, whether I ate pork or not, or ate fish on Friday, or wore sidelocks. Whoever made a trillion constellations move could not possibly be so nit-picking and small-souled as to create sulphur-eating horned devils with pitchforks boiling poor sinners in chemical vats for having fasted on the wrong day. God would respect me as I respected him. At any rate I would no longer be afraid of Him. I would not fry in hell.

Richard Erdoes

HOW SHALL I WRITE?
A Bedouin

A Bedouin
How shall I write ? What, what shall I write?

A friend
People want to know how you see the monks and the Israelis. What does a Moslem Bedouin think of Jews? . . . of Christians? The monks are not Moslem, after all, and neither are the Israelis. How are you, the Jebaliya . . .

A Bedouin (interrupting)
. . . connected? Why? I'll write in my language, Arabic. Still better, to make it easier, I'll put it on a tape and talk as if I am speaking to you, as if I'm telling you, my friend, a story. The Jebaliya and the monks and the Jebaliya and the Jews—Right?

I know how it was that we Jebaliya and Jews became close. Like us they love the mountains. They love the wadis and the orchards. We met right at the place loved by both people. You know there are so many other people who come and go to see the monastery. We have no contact with them at all. It's not the same with the Jews. Well, with them, we met in the place that we both love

The monk's religion and the Beduoin's religion are apart. So it should have been that they would not like each other. In fact, it is the opposite— they love each other. You see, the Jebaliya are easy-going about religions. There is no such problem as, "I am Moslem! You are Jew! You are Christian!" As long as we are together it is not that important. It is not impor-

120

tant enough for us to be in anger or fight.

For a long time now we have been living together with the Christians. Like brothers we have been living together, talking together, walking together . . .

We do not have this thing that because we are Moslem everybody else must be.

I am a Moslem for my own sake . . . not for them. As long as they are good to me.

Now when the Jews first came to Sinai we were really scared, but then they did not harm us. We hiked with them and worked together in the mountains and in construction work. As soon as the routine of life and the good experience came, it all settled very well. They saw us, you see, and our way of life and loved it.

It is strange. There are people who see us making orchards in these barren mountains and say, "These people are mad, they are sick in their minds to do this. This is a land of craziness." We get angry with such people. Everyone hates him who hates his country. But the Israelis fell in love with our mountains, and so we loved them.

There is this problem of monks and that they have no children. We think about it often. But we will never think or say the monks are mad, or are no good, because they do not marry. A woman is good for you and for your life, but marriage has its problems too, doesn't it? When you weigh advantage and loss you begin to realize the balance. There was this Russian Orthodox monk in the monastery some years ago who told me once about the way he saw it. He said: "Women interfere with prayer and you forget your faith. That's why it is worth it to not marry. Now you wake up in the morning and there is life, a taste to air . . . food. If you have a family your head is filled with problems of livelihood and provisions. Religion flies away."

This Alexander, the Russian, he liked us Bedouin. He used to come up to the mountains and stay with us. We would sit and take our time in the evenings, and talk. He was young, which helps. I sometimes feel a little shy with some of the older monks from the monastery.

I remember the first time I went to the monastery. It was with my father and we went to get some provisions from the monks. They gave me some presents and sweets. . . and I learned to call them "father"—"abuna". We just sat there talking. I kind of liked it then.

Our family, you know, has been in close touch with the monks since the time of my grandfather and his grandfather. There are some orchards in the mountains that we share owning with the monastery. But the way we look at it is not as if some monks used to be with our ancestors and then they died and others came. No, we see them all as one. Whoever comes as a monk—he is one and the same for us. And still we know them all by name. They are part of our life

I was twelve years old that time. We went into the church. You know how beautiful it is. You've seen it. It looks so fine and the incense smells sweet. Yes, I am a Moslem and do not pray in it. . . yet I love it.

Just like that.

Look, I really love the monastery as a whole and the monks. In the past they provided for us and we still do see the monastery as if it's also ours; not just their's. True, the tribe has grown, things are changing. Most people have jobs now outside the monastery which makes it look smaller to them. Some see it and say, "It has come to nothing." But for me, I love the monks and the monastery. Something that has been your father's and your grandfather's before it was yours. . . how can you turn away from it?

There are people who have trouble, who cannot sleep at night. They will go to the monastery and pray in the mosque inside the walls, and then go in the chapel. This is good for "Baraka" (blessing) . My aunt on my father's side once made this pilgrimage. She went with her husband, the late Sliman a Tesh. They spent the night in that little place dedicated to Elijah outside the monastery wall, and in the morning went inside the chapel to recieve the "Baraka." The source of the "Baraka" is in the holiness of the monks of the old time. They were wonderful, perfect!—so poor and so simple, and they loved our people. They worked the orchards with us and like us they owned nothing.

We are here in this desert; it is empty. . . and where there is nobody around you just have to be happy with whoever you get. If you were here with a monkey and no one else. . . we would have made a friend. This is just the way it is. All who live here in the desert must be friends . . . friends. This is what must be no matter what sects we are.

Say you and me walk this wadi and camp overnight. At dinner you want us to make fatir (flat loaves) and I want Libeh bread. So we make both, no hard feelings. But it is not always this way. There is "hzab" too—fanaticism. These are people who want everybody to be like them. A fanatic faction comes and commands that we all do like them or else they will shed our blood. With us Bedouin this cannot be. Each one must live according to his way. I, for example, hardly ever pray but my father never pushes me to pray or threatens me. I am free. In the same way, when I see someone eating pig's meat I am not mad with him. If he enjoys it . . . it is fine with me. But fanatics are not like this; and there are fanatics in each religion, not just Islam. I know this.

I think the reason is that people cannot talk.

Let me explain. Long ago people were like trees or animals. They had no interest in their fellows and just lived their lives in the earth. But then they started to discuss things between them. Say there is a path that goes through this valley and I don't know about it. If we talk, you'll tell me about it, won't you? This is the discussing that I mean. Whatever I know. . . I'll share with you.

Life is not long enough to find out everything about things alone. Sixty or seventy years are not enough, especially since everything keeps changing.

A person must take from others and give to them.

Life is not for the sake of war or argument; it is not for the sake of accusing each other. Only people's twisted brains have brought them to this . . .

This good kind of discussion has been going on between us and the monks for hundreds of years. They are Europeans, they are not familiar with the desert and the problems in it. We Jebaliya are responsible for them. We will tell them when people come from somewhere else and harm their properties in distant mountains. In return they gave us food.

Now this thing about the different religions.

Say I tell you I know this thing is black, and you say white. I could be hurt and mad with you, thinking you are doing harm to me in your mind. You make me feel useless or half-witted. In such a case we had better not talk again.

But if we can decide to sit and talk, maybe we can discuss things and see that really this thing is gray. We meet half way.

But then another problem. If we set out to talk and work together, there is danger that my father and my brothers and your family would not allow us. They say, "You are a Moslem. He is a Jew. You cannot be together." Then there is nothing but the mountains to escape to.

This kind of problem starts with infants. Children hear tall stories about people of other races. They hear that they kill without thought, that they drink blood, that they do wrong as a routine. I heard such things when I was growing up about the Jews. This made me think, "If I ever walk three meters with an Israeli, I'll have to kill him; no way around it." Now if I hadn't come to work with them and know them, my mind would still be in that state today. Children today, though, hear different stories. They hear from their parents how good it was with the Israelis—the work, the food, the money. And they hear other good things.

Once I provoked the elders of my religion by saying there was no God. And they said one thing I had to agree with.

They said, look at the world, look around . . . designed perfectly. Who made the mountains? Who made the earth and the world and the people in it? Look at the human being. He has eyes; he breathes. He has a nose so he can inhale and smell and be sure the food is good before he eats it, and so stay healthy. It is all made to some plan and someone had to prepare it all. It's not like a tree trunk brought down the valley by a flood—at random. When you see a wall made of stones . . . could anyone say it was put together by a bunch of stones that fell from the mountain?

I do not know the name for who did all that. But I know who did all that *is*.

But jealousy is a difficulty! This man has five children and they all hate each other. Each says, "My father is mine alone. He is not yours. The clothes and presents he brings are only for me, no one else." And so there is no love between them. That is how it is with religions—they all try to foresee, they all tell what will happen to whom: "You, you will go to heaven, you will go to hell, God does not care for you, God loves me !" This is how they try to control people. But truly only God has control.

A Bedouin
Sinai Peninsula
Egypt

"I AM A STRANGER IN THE LAND"
(Ps. 119:19)
Rabbi Michael Goldberg

Despite the divergencies among various biblical accounts of the tent meetings in the wilderness,[1] one storied element nevertheless remains the same throughout: each meeting takes place on unfamiliar territory and always between those who, as God and humankind, are irreducibly different from one another. Yet somehow, these recurring encounters with the foreign and the strange provide the indispensible condition for moving ever closer to the journey's promise.

Indeed, from the perspective of the Exodus, Israel's formative narrative in the light of which the wilderness trek is cast, to reject the alien simultaneously entails the embrace of consequences destructive of any promise that life may have:

> Now a new king arose over Egypt, who *did not know* Joseph. And he said to *his people,* "Look, *the Israelite* people are much too numerous for *us.* Let *us,* then, deal shrewdly with *them*, lest *they* increase and, in the event of war, join our enemies in fighting *against us* and gain ascendancy over the country. So *they* set taskmasters over *them* to oppress them with forced labor. . .[2]

These verses, repeatedly juxtaposing one people against the other, give voice to the rationale behind Pharaoh's subsequent oppression of Israel, namely, the perception of a fundamental—and irreconcilable—dichotomy between "us" and "them". The Israelites' tragic circumstance ultimately stems from their being viewed as those *not us*; as those who, no matter what previous contacts have occurred (i.e, ". . . When the famine became severe in the land of Egypt, Joseph laid open all that was with-thin, and apportioned grain to the Egyptians." Gen. 41:56), nonetheless remain forever them, and as such, are seen as *strangers eternally suspect and dangerous.* Consequently, it is not Israel's otherness *per se* that brings calamity upon her; rather it is the sheer *dread*[3] of that otherness which sets loose Egypt's violence and which, through the plagues, will eventually engender equal if not greater violence for Egypt also.[4]

But while the Exodus narrative depicts Pharaoh's horror of the stranger to be horribly doomed at the Sea of Reeds, later history nevertheless recounts such xenophobia resurfacing time and time again, and unfortunately, our own time proves no exception. And we need not invoke images of some dark, looming "foreign menace" to arouse our fears. We need only summon up our home-grown spectres as we consider, for example, the assumptions underlying many of our social contract theories, from Hobbes' *Leviathan* and ranging to Rawls' *Theory of Justice.* With their use of metaphors of "the state of nature" and the "veil of ignorance", such works ask us to envisage each other not simply as strangers, but more basically, as strangers whose interests and desires are so opposed to each other that unless they—and we—can be controlled, most likely we will all be at one another's throats. Ironically, "civil" society is said to spring from such a savage vision. Small wonder, then, that as Alasdair MacIntyre has observed, "Modern politics is civil war carried on by other means".[5]

Accordingly, it ought also come as no surprise that our judicial process has typically been characterized as an "adversary system", which now seems to grow increasingly litigious as persons with nothing mutual except mutual antipathy resort to show-downs between their "hired-gun" lawyers in the courtroom. In fact the obsession of contemporary ethics with the quasi-legal concept of "person" may well be an index of our present estrangement from one another. For if the prime locus of our notion of a person is the law court, then in using such a term to delineate our moral relationships, we imply that we engage each other first and foremost as adversarial claimants. If so, however, we ought take note of the somewhat perverse moral logic inherent in our discussions. In our arguments about abortion, euthanasia, and the like, while we try to settle the question of who is a person and who thus has legitimate rights—with correspondingly legitimate claims upon (i.e., against) us—we conversely decide as well the issue of who lacks such status, rights, and claims—and who therefore we can legitimately (i.e., *safely*) ignore. Stanley Hauerwas, commenting on the recent prominence of such reasoning in the field of medical ethics, has put the matter this way:

> In the literature of past medical ethics the notion of "person" does not seem to have played a prominent role in deciding how medicine should or should not be used vis-a-vis a particular patient. Why is it then that we suddenly seem so concerned with the question of whether someone is a person?

It is my hunch we have much to learn from this phenomenon as it is an indication, not that our philosophy of medicine or medical ethics is in good shape, but rather that it is in deep trouble. For it is my [view] that we are trying to put forward "person" as a regulative notion to direct our health care as substitute for what only a substantive community and story can do.[6]

As we moderns continually emphasize individual identity at the expense of communal identity, we similarly tend to abandon any hope of a shared story as the basis for our life together. Lacking such a common narrative, we can intersect one another's lives only as random persons, as potentially threatening antagonists, in short, as alienated strangers.[7]

And yet, who stands at the center of the core narrative jointly held by the Abrahamic faiths but the figure of that paradigmatic stranger, Abraham himself, who is "alien" throughout all his journeys.[8] If our shared root story spurs us to revere Abraham, it does so in no small part precisely because of what it is he fathers, namely, offspring like himself, i.e, nomadic outsiders such as son Ishmael and grandson Israel.[9] Thus, if we would place ourselves truly within Abraham's venerable (story) line, there is one story-piece we must venerate above all others: despite his status as thoroughgoing stranger in the world, Abraham bears no harm but only blessing for the world—"And you shall be a blessing. . . and in you all the families of the earth shall be blessed."[10]

No doubt, those of Pharaoh's mind, who see strangers harboring only malice and never boon, must regard an Abraham as utterly foreign and strange indeed, and they are left it seems with little choice but to erect the kind of unbridgeable barriers between 'us' and 'them' that almost inevitably lead to unspeakable acts of violence against 'them' by 'us'.[11] In the last analysis such violence perpetrated against the other also wreaks violence against the world, for it kills the very possibility of an meaningful talk about *a world* as a unified sphere of life. Yet it is just such a world that we would-be heirs of Abraham claim is the beneficiary of our ancestor's "godsend".

For those of us who would convey Abraham's story to the world, the reason that we can speak about a world in the first place is because our story schools us that all of what we call "the world" is in the first place formed by God. Whatever else we may have heard of God—and whatever else we may say of him—we must hear and say at least this much: he is the creator whose creatures' lives are all necessarily bound one to the other as part and parcel of the same creation. With all life thus inextricably connected from the start, though we may likely encounter strangers on our life ventures, we can never essentially encounter them as altogether *estranged* from us. To the extent that we do find ourselves estranged from others, then to that same extent we must find ourselves estranged from our community-forming narratives of Abraham and his

God.[12]

But the worst aspect of such estrangement may be simply this: in distancing ourselves from the stranger, we may just be distancing ourselves from other Abrahams carrying God's life-blessing promises to us.

According to the scriptural saga, the Tent of Meeting existed only in the wilderness, and yet precisely in that no-man's land, the Lord of all the Earth was made most manifest to humankind. And how could it have been otherwise? For in the end, as in the beginning, the earth is *no-man's* land, but only God's, on whose "turf" we are mere sojourners passing through—"For the land is Mine; you are but strangers residing with Me".[13]

Perhaps the world ought be best regarded as one great tent of meeting where we strangers come together and come upon that quintessential Other, who repeatedly beckons us forward toward the promised destination of our lives.

Rabbi Michael Goldberg
Collegeville, Minnesota

1. The exact relationship between the *ohel moed*—"tent of meeting"—and the *mishkan*—"the tabernacle"—is still a matter of dispute among scholars, who also disagree about the source or sources underlying each of these traditions. See Brevard Childs, *The Book of Exodus: A Critical, Theological Commentary* (Philadelphia: The Westminster Press, 1974), pp. 357-9, 529-37.

2. Ex. 1:8-11; NJPS translation; italics mine.

3. Ex. 1:9; Heb. vayakutzu.

4. For a fuller discussion of this point, see my book, *Jews and Christians, Getting Our Stories Straight* (Nashville: Abingdon Press, 1985)

5. Alasdair MacIntyre, *After Virtue* (Notre Dame, Ind.: University of Notre Dame Press, 1981), p. 236 .

6. Stanley Hauerwas, *Truthfulness and Tragedy* (Notre Dame, Ind.: University of Notre Dame Press, 1977), pp 127-8.

7. Cf. Alfred Schutz, "The Stranger," *Collected Papers*, 3 vols.(The Hague: Nijhoff, 1964).

8. See, for example, Gen. 23:4.

9. See, e.g., Gen. 12:1,5-10; 15:13; 16:11-12; 21:14; 28:13-22; 46:1-4. Interestingly, at some level, *all* our children are strangers in our midst in the sense that they come to us from only God-knows-where, frequently confronting us with only God-knows-what.

10. Gen. 12:2,3.

11. See Ex. 1:11,13-14,22, where Pharaoh's policies escalate from corvee labor to enslavement to genocide. In this regard, there is an eerie similarity between the implementation of Pharaoh's program against Israel and that of Hitler against the Jews. For in both cases, an initial demarcation of these "outsiders" as totally "other" is followed by a policy of total extinction of those others.

12. Significantly, the Torah's well-known repeated stress on regard for strangers suggests that were Israel to turn her back on these outsiders in her midst, she would *ipso facto* turn her back on her own history and identity as well.

13. Lev. 26:23.

THE SAME MESSAGE REPEATED

Mohammed H. El-Zayyat

I

In the year six hundred and ten after Jesus Christ, some of the followers of the then new religion of Islam escaped to East Africa from persecution in their homeland. When the Negus (Emperor) of Ethiopia had listened attentively to the group seeking refuge in his country as they explained their new religion, he wisely commented that their religion seemed to have sources in common with his own Christian faith. He was right in discerning this link. The new religion's Holy Book, the Koran, states very clearly and repeatedly that its divine message was the same as that "preached before by Jesus Christ and before that by Moses and by Abraham and by Noah."[1] In the Koran, Abraham is called "Khalil Allah"(God's friend); Moses is called "Kalim Allah" (God's interlocutor); Jesus is "Kalimatu Allah" (God's word), while Mohamed was "Rasoul Allah', or God's messenger. He redelivered their same divine message. God was one and eternal. His message to man could not be but the same.

II

The message of Mohamed reasserted these ideals of freedom, equality, and human brotherhood.

The divine message was, however, always received by men, by mortals. Men could corrupt the message. They could and would deviate to tribal and racial pride. They could and would deny the brotherhood of humanity. The strong would again subjugate the weak and the rich would again exploit the poor. Excessive zeal can betray the divine message. A man may accept God's message only in name, but live and behave unconcerned with its ideals.

Men were created free. Men inherited no sin. It was they who would commit their own sins, or achieve their own good deeds.

Men were born equal. "All men came from Adam and Adam came from dust." The Koran stated, "there was no room for false feelings of superiority because of colour, race or parenthood . . . No Arab shall be considered better than a non-Arab;" It also asserts that, "Only a man's good deeds would elevate him over another." All human beings were created by God. They were His children; therefore, brethren.

Those were the ideals of freedom, equality and the brotherhood of humanity[2] that the message of Islam reasserted. One who believes in these ideals and behaves according to them should fear no one and no power on earth. God's power was greater than any other. The cry of "Allahu Akbar," or "God is greater," assures the believer of that simple fact.

The message of Islam aimed at creating a society of good human beings believing in freedom, in equality, and in working for the common good of humanity. Such a call was of course to be violently resisted by all who did not, and all who do not, believe in those ideals.

IV

The message of Mohamed did not die with his death in the summer of the year six hundred and thirty-two (A.D.). There were then a score of people around his deathbed and a few hundred in his primitively built mosque waiting for a new leader to lead their prayers. When Mohamed died, the call of Islam had reached the south and north of Arabia, but had hardly been accepted outside it. Only one hundred years later Moslems were fighting the battle of Poitiers in France. There are now some eight hundred million Moslems, double their number twenty years ago.[3] They live in all the five continents and their mosques are to be found not only in the towns and villages of Asia and Africa but also in the capitals of Europe, the Americas and of Australia. They are all required—by their religion to assert their belief in strict monotheism by declaring that there is no god but the one God (Allah)[4] and that Mohamed is His messenger. They are required to fast the month of Ramadan (from sunrise to sunset). They are required to give specified alms to the deserving. They are asked to make the pilgrimage, once in a lifetime, to Mecca—where Abraham, the Muslims believe, had built his house—if possible, and they are required to make their prayers to God five times a day.

* * * *

The hundreds of millions of Moslems end those daily prayers with an appeal to God to "bless Mohamed and his people" as He had blessed "Abraham and his people."

The people of Abraham, the hundreds of millions of Moslems believe, are those who have accepted the divine message he brought, the message that was brought to them again by Moses and by Jesus and by Mohamed, the same message preaching liberty, equality and the brotherhood of humanity.

Mohamed H. El-Zayyat
Deputy for Damietta,
The National Assembly
Egypt.

1. The Koran affirms in thirteen different places, e.g., Surat II Ayat 131 that its revelation was already contained in all monotheistic religions before it (especially the Torah and the Evangile).

2. Koran Surat XLIX Ayat 10

3. Unofficial statistics give the number of Moslems at 400 million in 1967, 700 million in 1979, and more than 800 million in 1985.

4. The Arabic word Allah is compounded of the article al (the) and the word ILAH, meaning God. Allah simply means, The God.

LISTEN ISRAEL
André Chouraque

When Jesus defined the first commandment he referred to the passage from Deuteronomy which constituted the declaration of faith of the Synagogue: "Listen Israel, the Lord our God the Lord is One, and you will love the Lord your God with all your heart, with all your soul and with all your might."

In this phrase, one of the most glorious, without doubt, of all Revelation, not a word is too much, not one word could be cut from what preceded or followed; we are in the presence of the fullness of verbal meaning, and the spirit is abashed before the flamboyant intensity of these simple words.

"Listen..." Is it superfluous to notice it? To listen is first of all to be quiet, to know how to be quiet; to create in oneself this empty place, this availability which allows us to welcome the other. The farther away the other the deeper must be the silence so it is possible to hear it. And when the Other calls itself the Lord, the Absolute, absolute, royal, it must be the silence that welcomes. To be silent before God is not only to stop up one's lips but to secure the peace of all the senses, the harmony of body and soul both poised and tensed in this marvelous pause where the voice of the Other is becoming present.

To be silent is also to accept oneself as a creature, to go past obedience and reach the abandonment of one's self to the will of God. It is to tender oneself to, and not separate from the Other; to not divorce from his order, and to remain his faithful ally always available and free.

This demands the true silence of passion, desire, pride; this slow climb in oneself toward that clear look which permits true discernment. This rebirth is in the purity of the act contemplated for the sake that the Other will be known solitarily, not for oneself, not for oneself . . .

The Silence is to depart from all duality in order to open oneself entirely to the call of the Other, as Israel rose up and called itself at the call of the Lord. It is such a silence that permits God to call himself in our soul and permits us to recognize The One who is Our God, The One with whom one ceases to be a wolf for a man, the one who triumphs over the Adversity and casts a bridge between all, whose order is to create fraternity among all without limit and without end. For he is the Unique, one in Himself, one in his Creation, One in his will. And my silence before him is not full, is not true until he makes my will identical with His will. Oh that he would take away my natural duality to throw me on this slope, on the extreme edge of the creation, where the existent renounces itself in the ocean of an infinite glory!

I am only a believer so far as I do not ravage this unity of God, of the Creation. When His will ceases to be my will I here am sinking in idolatry, unity ceases to be mine, I am plunged into falsity and appearances; my silence was unable to make itself so deep that no voice had the force to penetrate it beside the beloved's.

The Unique One suddenly appears, just so, in the bosom of silence that welcomes him, and that he penetrates with his own praise. The divine symphony continues: "Listen Israel, the Lord our God, the Lord is One, and you shall love the Lord your God . . ."

After the name of the One has been pronounced is not all said? Has not utterance exhausted its final resources? One word is still possible, one word remains necessary; it emerges from the unity without other—love.

The silence permits the manifestation of the One, leaves to his voice of holding back in the soul, but the soul does not realize his presence in Him except by love. It is nothing to know that God is One and the creation One if I separate myself, if I exalt myself apart from this unity; and the touch-stone, the sword which judges me, is love. In truth there is more in this word than a command: it is a confirmation unfolding, growing with the silence if I am absolutely quiet, I am Israel, I hear the Lord, I know that he is ours, I know that he is One and already my soul is totally vanquished by love. It is no longer necessary to say it to myself because already, I love.

And love operates the final metamorphosis. God is no longer the God of merely all, whom I knew at the start of my silence. The biblical word pierces me: "You will love the Lord your God . . ." like your father or your spouse. Love in its flame can not be distinguished from him . . . and in this fire all passes: ". . . with all your heart, with all your soul and with all your might"

"All my heart, all my soul all my might . . ." But what is left of me?" "Nothing." "Nothing?" Nothing. The Realm of Silence . . .

André Chouraqui
Jerusalem

BIOGRAPHIES

Michael Baron is the director of the Lindisfarme Mountain Retreat in Colorado.

Mother Tessa Bielecki is co-foundress of the Spiritual Life Institute. As Mother Abbess of the community, she has led a monastic life of solitude and silence for the past eighteen years. As an "apostolic hermit," she also shares her contemplative life by teaching, leading retreats, speaking at ecumenical conferences, and editing *Desert Call,* the Institute's quarterly magazine.

Lynne Bundesen is the author of the syndicated column *On Religion*, and a woman with deep personal experience in American spirituality.

André Chouraqui is a writer, historian and poet. He received a gold medal from l'Academie Francaise for his translation of the Bible. This work is published as *L'Univers de la Bible.* For many years he served as deputy mayor of Jerusalem.

Richard Erdoes is an author of many books but most well known for his work in Native American studies. He is author of *Lame Deer,* and most recently in collaboration with Alfonso Ortiz, *American Indian Myths and Legends.*

Michael Goldberg is a rabbi and the first holder of a recently endowed chair in Jewish Theology at St. John's University, Collegeville, Minnesota.

Sheikh Mohammed Sayad Al Jemal Al Rafai Ash-Shadhulli is a leader of the Shadhulli dervish order. The center of his activity is in Jerusalem.

Dr. Vera John-Steiner received her Ph.D. from the University of Chicago. She is a psychologist specializing in language who has been widely published in psycholinguistic journals. Her new book, *Notebooks of the Mind* will be published by the University of New Mexico Press in November 1985.

Sahag Kalaydjian is the librarian and teacher of liturigal music at the Armenian Patriarchate of Jerusalem.

Father William McNamara has been a Discalced Carmelite monk for years. He is a well-known lecturer and retreat master, the founder of the Spiritual Life Institute and the author of a number of books, most recently and noteworthy, *Mystical Passion* (Paulist Press) and *Earthy Mysticism* (Crossroad).

Paul Mendes-Flohr is Professor of Modern Jewish Thought at the Hebrew University in Jerusalem. He recently has edited two books of Martin Buber's writings, *Land of Two Peoples* and *Ecstatic Confessions: The Heart of Mysticism.*

John Menken is a playwright and community planner and editor of *The Tent of Meeting Texts.*

Dan Rabinowitz is an anthropologist who has worked with the *Society of the Protection of Nature in Israel.* He has spent considerable time living in the vicinity of Jebel Musa which has traditionally been identified as Mt. Sinai.

Father Hilary Thimmesh is a Benedictine monk of wide accomplishment and many years of contemplative experience. Currently he is president of St. John's University, Collegeville, Minnesota.

Marina Warner is the author of a number of books including *Alone of All Her Sex* and *Joan of Arc.* The work included in this volume is a chapter from her new book *Eyes of Tiresias.*

Colin Williams was formerly Dean of Yale University Divinity School. Currently he is Vice-President of the Aspen Institute.

Mohammed H. El-Zayyat is Member of Parliament for his home district in Egypt. Formerly he served as Egypt's Foreign Minister. For many years he was among the closest pupils of Taha Husein, who though little known in the West, was in the opinion of the editor one of this century's great human beings.

NOTES